iPHONE™ & iPOD® TOUCH
QuickSteps

About the Author

Dwight Spivey is the author of several technical books, including *How to Do Everything: Mac*, first and second editions. He is also a software and support engineer for Konica Minolta, where he specializes in working with Mac operating systems, applications, and hardware, as well as color and monochrome laser printers. He teaches classes on Mac usage, writes training and support materials for Konica Minolta, and has been a beta tester for Mac OS X since its first incarnation. Dwight lives on the Gulf Coast of Alabama with his wife, Cindy, and their three beautiful children, Victoria, Devyn, and Emi. Frequently a test dummy for his kids, he also studies theology, draws comic strips, and roots for the Auburn Tigers in his ever-decreasing spare time.

About the Technical Editor

Guy Hart-Davis is the author of *How to Do Everything: iPod®, iPhone™ & iTunes®, Fifth Edition* and *Mac OS® X Leopard™ QuickSteps*.

iPHONE™ & iPOD® TOUCH

QuickSteps

DWIGHT SPIVEY

New York Chicago San Francisco
Lisbon London Madrid Mexico City
Milan New Delhi San Juan
Seoul Singapore Sydney Toronto

The McGraw·Hill Companies

Cataloging-in-Publication Data is on file with the Library of Congress

McGraw-Hill books are available at special quantity discounts to use as premiums and sales promotions, or for use in corporate training programs. To contact a representative, please e-mail us at bulksales@mcgraw-hill.com.

iPHONE™ & iPOD® TOUCH QUICKSTEPS

1234567890   CCI CCI   019

ISBN   978-0-07-163485-4
MHID   0-07-163485-1

SPONSORING EDITOR / Megg Morin

EDITORIAL SUPERVISOR / Jody McKenzie

PROJECT MANAGER / Vasundhara Sawhney, Glyph International

ACQUISITIONS COORDINATOR / Meghan Riley

TECHNICAL EDITOR / Guy Hart-Davis

COPY EDITOR / Lisa McCoy

PROOFREADER / Julie Searls

INDEXER / Valerie Perry

PRODUCTION SUPERVISOR / George Anderson

COMPOSITION / Glyph International

ILLUSTRATION / Glyph International and Filip Yip

ART DIRECTOR, COVER / Jeff Weeks

COVER DESIGNER / Pattie Lee

SERIES CREATORS / Marty and Carole Matthews

SERIES DESIGN / Bailey Cunningham

To my sister Kelli, brother-in-law Keith, and
their beautiful children, Kelsey, Keaton, Kelen, and
Kooper. I love and thank God for my Flemings!

Contents at a Glance

Chapter 1 **Getting to Know Your iPhone 3G/iPod touch**..................1
Understand the interface; use Sleep/Wake; lock and protect the
device; use Home; use the touchscreen and keyboard

1

Chapter 2 **Configuring and Syncing Your Device with iTunes**....... 13
Sync your device with iTunes; set sync options; understand the various
panes; name your device; create ringtones; subscribe to podcasts

2

Chapter 3 **Making Calls with Your iPhone 3G**........................ 31
Make calls; use contacts; place calls on hold; assign ringtones;
handle multiple calls; use Visual Voicemail; create a greeting

3

Chapter 4 **Communicating with Mail**.. 43
Add e-mail accounts; configure email settings; use multiple accounts;
view and organize e-mail; view attachments; modify font settings

4

Chapter 5 **Surfing the Web with Safari**.................................... 55
View web pages; bookmark favorite sites; change the default search
engine; manage bookmarks; utilize RSS feeds; save web images

5

Chapter 6 **Enjoying Music and Video**...................................... 67
Use the iTunes interface; import audio; use the iTunes Store; sync
music and podcasts; create playlists; format movies; organize media

6

Chapter 7 **Taking and Managing Photos**.............................. 85
Take pictures; sync photos; upload photos; create slideshows;
e-mail photos; send photos via MMS; assign photos to contacts

7

Chapter 8 **Using Applications that Make Your Life Easier**.. 103
Get weather forecasts; use Notes; use Clock; send and receive text
messages; get directions; find local businesses; track appointments

8

Chapter 9 **Modifying Settings**... 123
Use Airplane Mode; connect to a Wi-Fi network; utilize a VPN; adjust
sound and brightness; configure wallpaper; connect to a television

9

Chapter 10 **Getting to Know the App Store**........................... 145
Find apps; view paid and free apps; search for specific apps; install
and update apps; delete apps from your device; submit reviews

10

Index 169

Contents

Acknowledgments...xiv

Introduction xv

Chapter 1 **Getting to Know Your iPhone 3G/iPod touch**...1

Learn Your Device's Hardware...2
   Discover the iPhone 3G Features..2
   Discover the iPod touch Features..2

Use the Sleep/Wake Button..3
   Turn Your Device On and Off...3
   Lock and Unlock Your Device...3
   Protect Your Device with a Passcode.......................................4

Understand the Home Screen...5
   Using Multiple Home Screens..7
   Utilize the Home Button...7
   Navigate with the Touchscreen...7
   Double-click the Home Button...8
   Use the Onscreen Keyboard...8
   Customizing Icons in the Dock...10
   Arrange Icons...10
   Resetting the Default Icons...11

Charge Your Device...12

Chapter 2 **Configuring and Syncing
Your Device with iTunes**.....................................13

   Checking if iTunes Is Already Installed....................................14

Get iTunes..14

Synchronize Your Device...15
   Register Your Device with iTunes..16
   View Your Device in iTunes...16

Set Sync Options..16
   Understand the Summary Pane...17
   Preventing Automatic Syncing with All Devices.........................18
   Grasp the Info Pane...20
   Naming Your Device..21
   What Is MobileMe?...21
   Decipher the Ringtones Pane 23
   Understand the Music and Videos Panes.................................25
   Creating Your Own Ringtones...26
   Use the Photos Pane...26
   Make Sense of the Podcasts Pane...27
   Grasp the Applications Pane...27
   Subscribing to Podcasts..29

3 Chapter 3 **Making Calls with Your iPhone 3G** 31

Understand the Phone Buttons 32
Use Basic Call Features 32
    Make a Quick Call with the Keypad 32
    Use Contacts to Make a Call 33
    Receive a Call 33
    ⚙ Using the Keypad During a Call 34
    Place a Call on Hold or Mute 34
    Use the Speaker 34
Work with Contacts 35
    Create New Contacts Manually 35
    Create a Contact from a Recent Call 36
    Utilize Favorites 36
Advanced Call Features 37
    ⚙ Assigning Ringtones to Contacts 37
    Silence Incoming Calls 37
    Handle Multiple Calls 38
    Utilize Visual Voicemail 40
    ⚙ Changing Your Greeting 41
    Browse Recent Calls 41
    Use Other iPhone Applications During a Call 42

4 Chapter 4 **Communicating with Mail** 43

Setting Up E-mail 43
    Add an E-mail Account 44
    ⊘ Discovering Exchange Servers 45
    Configure Accounts 45
    ⚙ Configuring Your Account's SMTP Server 46
    ⚙ Removing an Account 47
    Utilize More Than One Account 47
Use Your E-mail Account 48
    Check for New Mail 48
    See the Contents of E-mails 49
    ⚙ Setting the Number of Messages Shown 50
    View E-mail Attachments 50
    Delete E-mail 51
    ⚙ Deleting Multiple E-mails 52
    Move E-mail to Other Mailboxes or Folders 52
    Empty the Trash 52
    Reply to and Forward E-mails 53
    Create New E-mails 53
    ⚙ Adding a Signature to Outgoing E-mails 54
    Configure E-mail Fonts 54

5 Chapter 5 **Surfing the Web with Safari** 55

Safari Basics 56
    Understand Safari's Interface 56
    View Web Pages 56
    ⊘ Using Specialized iPhone/iPod touch Web Sites 57
    Enter an Address in the URL Field 57
    ⚙ Zooming In and Out of Pages 58
    Navigate Web Pages 58

Closing a Web Page 59
    Handle Multiple Browser Pages 59
    Choose a Default Search Engine 59
Utilize Bookmarks 60
    Create New Bookmarks 60
    Open a Site with a Bookmark 61
    Manage Your Bookmarks 61
Editing Bookmarks 62
    Use the History List 62
Clearing the History List 63
Advanced Safari 63
    Get the Latest News with RSS Feeds 63
    Save an Image to Your Device 64
Calling Phone Numbers Listed on Web Pages 64
    Use Web Clips on the Home Screen 64

Chapter 6   **Enjoying Music and Video** 67
Using iTunes 67
Learning More About iTunes 68
    Understand the iTunes Interface 68
    Import Audio into iTunes 69
Viewing Your Library with Cover Flow 70
Adding Lyrics to Your Songs 71
    Check Out the iTunes Store 72
    Subscribe to Podcasts 72
Continuing Your Education with iTunes U 73
    Sync Music with iTunes 74
    Create Playlists 75
Turning On Genius Playlists 76
    Create Smart Playlists 76
Copying Playlists to Your Device 77
    Format Movies for the iPhone/iPod touch with iTunes 77
    Rent or Buy Movies from the iTunes Store 77
    Sync Video with iTunes 78
Enjoy Media on Your iPhone 3G/iPod touch 79
    Browse Playlists, Artists, and Songs 79
    Organize Albums, Audiobooks, Compilations,
        Composers, Genres, and Podcasts 80
Downloading Podcasts with Your iPhone 3G/iPod touch 81
    Understand the Playback Controls 81
Configuring the Toolbar 82
    Browse Your Music with Cover Flow 82
    Watch Video on Your iPhone 3G/iPod touch 83

Chapter 7   **Taking and Managing Photos** 85
Become an iPhone Paparazzi 86
    Take Pictures with the Camera 86
    Record Video with the Camera 86
    View Your Pictures and Videos 87
Move Your Pictures and Videos to a Computer 88
    Sync Your Photos with a Computer Using iTunes 88
    Import Photos and Videos to a Mac Using iPhoto 90

Manually Import Photos and Videos to a Computer 92
Add Photo Albums with iPhoto 94
Add Photos and Videos to a MobileMe Gallery.................................95
Work with Pictures and Videos on Your Device.................................97
Sharing an Album on MobileMe 98
View a Slideshow 98
Setting Slideshow Preferences 99
Playing Music with Your Slideshow 99
E-mail a Photo or Video 99
Send a Photo or Video via SMS or MMS...99
Adding a Picture Within a Contact Record......................................100
Assign a Photo to a Contact 100
Set a Picture as Wallpaper 100
Taking Screen Shots 101
Delete Unwanted Pictures and Videos 101

8   Chapter 8   Using Applications that Make Your Life Easier 103

Apps for Everyday Life...103
Get Today's Forecast with Weather 104
Viewing Temps in Fahrenheit or Celsius..105
Getting More Information About a Location 106
Organize Your Thoughts with Notes 106
Manage Your Time with Clock 107
Communicate with Messages 110
Get Where You're Going with Maps 111
Viewing Satellite Images 112
Using Location Services with Your Device 113
Finding Your Current Location 114
Finding a Local Business 116
Add It All Up with Calculator 116
Watch Videos with YouTube 117
Apps that Keep You Productive..118
Keep Up (and Down) with Your Stocks 118
Track Appointments with Calendar 119
Manage Contacts...120
Searching for Items on Your Device 121
Create Reminders with Voice Memos 121

9   Chapter 9   Modifying Settings 123

Communication and Customization...123
Saving Battery Life by Enabling Airplane Mode 124
Utilize Airplane Mode (iPhone Only) 124
Modify Wi-Fi Settings 124
Ending Annoying Network Requests 126
Configure VPN Connections 126
Select Alternate Cellular Carriers (iPhone Only) 126
View Notifications 126
Set Up Sounds (iPhone Only) 127
Adjust Brightness...129
Change Wallpaper (iPhone Only)..129

🖉 Finding Cool Wallpaper on the Web 130
    Configure General Settings 130
🖉 Using Multiple-Language Keyboards 134
Application Settings..135
    Modify Mail, Contacts, and Calendars 135
    Adjust Phone Settings (iPhone Only) 138
    Modify Safari 140
    Customize Receiving Messages 141
    Personalize iPod (iPhone) or Music and Video (iPod touch) 141
🖉 Watching iPhone/iPod touch Videos on Your Television 143
    View Slideshows of Photos 143
    Sign In to the iTunes Store 143

Chapter 10 **Getting to Know the App Store** 145

Use the App Store on Your iPhone 3G/iPod touch...................................146
    Find Featured Applications 146
    Browse Categories for Applications...147
🖉 Using Paid or Free Apps? 148
    Check Out the Top 25 Paid and Free Apps 149
🖉 Finding App Reviews Online 150
    Search for Specific Applications 150
    Install a New App 150
    Update Currently Installed Applications.....................................152
    Delete Apps from Your Device 153
🔍 Syncing Purchased or Downloaded Apps 154
Utilize the App Store within iTunes...154
    Understand the App Store Interface 155
    Easily Find the Latest and Greatest Apps 159
🔍 Browsing to Quickly Find Specific Apps.......................................160
    Submit Reviews of Your Favorite (and Not-So-Favorite) Apps.............160
    Discover a Few of My Favorite Applications and Games 162
🖉 Jailbreaking the iPhone/iPod touch..167

....169

Acknowledgments

My biggest shout-out must go to Megg Morin, my patient, wise, and exceedingly kind sponsoring editor for this project. Thanks for putting your trust in me, Megg!

A very special thanks also goes to my acquisitions coordinator, Meghan Riley, and editorial supervisor, Jody McKenzie. Thank you both for keeping me on my toes and for making this whole project run so smoothly.

Many heartfelt thanks to my wonderful agent, Carole McClendon at Waterside. We scored again, Carole!

Guy Hart-Davis was once again my trusted voice of conscience and reason (aka technical editor) for this project. This is but one of several books we've collaborated on, and he is always a joy to work with.

I would also like to extend my sincere appreciation to the rest of the editorial and production staff (special thanks to Vasundhara Sawhney at Glyph) who made this book possible. You make my work seem a hundred times better than it really is. I have nothing but love for the good folks at McGraw-Hill!

Introduction

iPhone™ & iPod® touch QuickSteps will help you to learn the ins and outs of your iPhone 3G, iPhone 3GS, or iPod touch by breaking down the learning process into small, easy-to-follow steps.

Each chapter covers a specific topic, and several tasks are contained within each topic. These tasks help you discover basics such as setting up e-mail accounts and making phone calls, to more advanced items such as viewing e-mail attachments and juggling multiple calls at once. While you're certainly free to read the book from cover to cover, some readers may already be versed on certain aspects of the iPhone and iPod touch and want to move on to other topics they are not as familiar with. A quick perusal of the Table of Contents will list the tasks, or "How To's," covered in each chapter, allowing you to quickly find a topic of immediate interest.

Throughout each chapter you will find other elements such as Notes, Tips, and Cautions. These elements offer ways to help you better utilize a feature or perform a task in the chapter, as well as what things to be wary of when working with your device. Notes, Tips, and Cautions are placed on the page in such a manner as to not detract from the major steps provided for a given task, which helps keep you focused on the business at hand.

Each chapter is color-coded as well, and uses tabs on the edge of the pages to help differentiate topics from one another. Along with the color-coded tabs, the full-color images help you quickly identify items on the screen of your iPhone or iPod touch with those contained in the book.

It is my sincere desire to provide you with the best instruction possible for quickly familiarizing yourself with your iPhone or iPod touch. Happy QuickStepping!

Conventions Used in This Book

iPhone™ & iPod® touch QuickSteps uses several conventions designed to make the book easier for you to follow. Among these are

- A 🖉 in the Table of Contents or the How-To list in each chapter references a QuickFacts sidebar.

- A 🔍 in the Table of Contents or the How-To list in each chapter references a QuickSteps sidebar.

- **Bold type** is used for words on the screen that you are to do something with, such as click **Save As** or **Open**.

- *Italic* type is used for a word or phrase that is being defined or otherwise deserves special emphasis.

- <u>Underlined type</u> is used for text that you are to type from the keyboard. SMALL CAPITAL LETTERS are used for keys on the keyboard such as **ENTER** and **SHIFT**.

- When you are expected to enter a command, you are told to press the key(s). If you are to enter text or numbers, you are told to type them. Specific letters or numbers to be entered will be underlined.

- When you need to perform a menu command, you will be told, "Click File | Open."

How to…

- *Discover the iPhone 3G Features*
- *Discover the iPod touch Features*
- *Turn Your Device On and Off*
- *Lock and Unlock Your Device*
- *Protect Your Device with a Passcode*
- *Using Multiple Home Screens*
- *Utilize the Home Button*
- *Navigate with the Touchscreen*
- *Double-clicking the Home Button*
- *Use the Onscreen Keyboard*
- *Customizing Icons in the Dock*
- *Arrange Icons*
- *Resetting the Default Icons*

Chapter 1

Getting to Know Your iPhone 3G/iPod touch

You hold in your hands one of the hottest pieces of technology this side of NASA: the iPhone 3G, iPhone 3GS, or an iPod touch. Holding it in your hand is not good enough, though; you need to know how to use this little wonder. Your iPhone 3G(S) or iPod touch is able to do so much more than you may realize, including making phone calls (iPhone only), sending and receiving e-mail, playing games, and managing your life.

In this chapter we will cover the basics of operating your Apple handheld device, including learning how to turn your device on and off, familiarizing yourself with the touchscreen and its interface, and discovering what those neat little icons are on the touchscreen. For the sake of simplicity, we will refer to both the iPhone 3G and iPhone 3GS as "iPhone 3G" throughout the remainder of the book.

2 3 4 5 6 7 8 9 10

Headset jack   SIM card tray   Sleep/Wake button

Receiver
(phone
speaker)

Ring/Silent
switch

Camera (on back)

Volume buttons

Touchscreen

Home button

Speaker   Dock connector   Microphone

Figure 1-1: *The iPhone 3G's feature layout*

Learn Your Device's Hardware

Before you fire up that iPhone 3G or iPod touch, you may want to get the lay of the hardware land. One of the key features of both devices is the dearth of buttons. The iPhone 3G has only four buttons (actually there are three buttons and a switch), and the iPod touch sports just three. This lack of buttons is the most glaring physical difference from other competitive devices on the market. Let's have a quick glance at each device's physical layout.

Wi-Fi
antenna

Sleep/Wake
button

Volume
buttons

Touchscreen

Home
button

Dock connector   Headphones port

Figure 1-2: *The iPod touch's layout is a little different from that of the iPhone 3G.*

Discover the iPhone 3G Features

The iPhone 3G has three buttons and one switch, which allow you to perform multiple functions when used individually or in conjunction with other buttons. Figure 1-1 points out the technical layout of the iPhone 3G.

Discover the iPod touch Features

As mentioned, the iPod touch has one fewer button than the iPhone 3G, but most of your interaction with the device will take place on the touchscreen and utilizing the Home button. Figure 1-2 points out the major landmarks of the iPod touch to help you familiarize yourself with the device.

*Figure 1-3: **The default Home screen of the iPhone 3G.***

Use the Sleep/Wake Button

The Sleep/Wake button on the top of your device is used to turn it on or off, as well as to lock the device when not in use. You can also assign a passcode to your device, which protects it from prying eyes (and fingers). Also, when the device is locked, nothing will happen if you touch the touchscreen, which is especially helpful if you keep your device in a pocket or purse, for example.

Turn Your Device On and Off

To turn on your device, simply hold down the **Sleep/Wake** button for a few seconds until you see the Apple logo. Once the device powers all the way up, you will see the Home screen (Figure 1-3), which we will discuss a bit later in this chapter.

You seldom need to turn off your device; you typically will just lock it and let it sleep when not in use. Here's how to turn off your device when you need to:

1. Hold down the **Sleep/Wake** button for several seconds until you see the red slider button containing a white arrow at the top of the screen.

2. Press your finger on the red arrow, and drag the slider button all the way to the right of the screen to turn the device completely off.

   –Or–

   Press the **Cancel** button at the bottom of the screen if you change your mind about powering down.

Lock and Unlock Your Device

When your iPhone 3G or iPod touch is locked, it prevents tasks from being initiated by erroneously touching the touchscreen. To lock the device, press the **Sleep/Wake** button and quickly release it. The touchscreen will immediately go blank, but don't worry—the device is just in a sleep mode and isn't powered off.

NOTE

Turning off your iPhone will cause incoming calls to go directly to your voice mail.

NOTE

Even when they are locked, the iPhone is always listening for new calls and text messages, and both the iPhone and iPod touch are on the constant lookout for new e-mails.

Lock icon

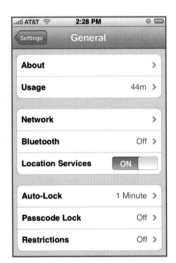

Figure 1-4: **The lock icon at the top of the screen indicates the device is locked.**

To unlock the device:

1. Press and release the **Home** button (more on that in a moment) or the **Sleep/Wake** button.
2. Drag the slider located at the bottom of the screen to unlock the device and open the touchscreen to your Home screen (Figure 1-4).

Protect Your Device with a Passcode

If you use an iPhone or iPod touch, it's a foregone conclusion that you use a personal computer, whether it's a Mac or a Windows-based PC. Since you are familiar with a computer, you most likely understand the need for security in some settings. Your iPhone 3G/iPod touch is basically a miniaturized computer, and since you will be storing personal information on it, you will most likely want to secure it from those who may accidentally, or even purposefully, wreak havoc with said information. Apple allows you to assign a passcode to your device, which is essentially a password for accessing the device once it's been locked.

1. Touch the **Settings** icon on your Home screen.
2. Select General, and touch **Password Lock**, seen near the bottom of Figure 1-5.
3. Enter a passcode by touching the buttons that correspond to the numbers you want to use (Figure 1-6).
4. Re-enter the passcode to verify it.
5. The Passcode Lock window opens (Figure 1-7), affording you several options for customizing the security of your device. Table 1-1 gives a brief explanation of the options in the Passcode Lock window.

Figure 1-5: **The General screen takes you to the Passcode Lock settings.**

Figure 1-6: **Use a four-digit number to secure your device with a passcode.**

CAUTION

Do not lose your passcode! If you forget your passcode and have enabled the Erase Data option, you can lose all the data on your device after 10 failed attempts at entering the passcode. You can recover your device by syncing it with iTunes if you have created a backup. See Chapter 2 for information on syncing your device.

OPTION	FUNCTION
Turn Passcode Off	Disables the passcode currently in use. Touch the field on your device's screen, and enter the passcode to disable it.
Change Passcode	Aptly named, this option allows you to modify the passcode you are currently using. Just touch the field, enter your old passcode, and then enter the new one.
Require Passcode	Allows you to set the length of time the device is idle before it requires you to enter the passcode. This is helpful if you lock and unlock your device often (you won't have to enter the passcode repeatedly); but the longer the time interval you set, the more vulnerable your device's data will be. Touch the field and select the desired time (I suggest you leave it at the default, which is Immediately, for security's sake).
Erase Data	Turning this option to On will cause all the data on your device to be erased after 10 unsuccessful attempts at entering the passcode.

*Table 1-1: **Passcode Lock Customization Options Explained***

Figure 1-7: **Customize the security of your iPhone 3G or iPod touch.**

Figure 1-8: **Items on the Home screen.**

Understand the Home Screen

The Home screen is your base of operations and is where all the action is. The Home screen's layout is simple and to the point, providing you with essential information for keeping up with some of your device's options and features. From the Home screen, you can open any application on your device; whenever you close an application, you are taken immediately back to the Home screen.

Table 1-2 lists the applications that come standard on the iPhone 3G and the iPod touch. Most of the applications reside on both devices, but some are particular to a single device. Each will be covered in depth in later chapters.

The layout of items on the Home screen is almost identical on both devices. Figure 1-8 shows the typical lay of the land (the iPhone 3G Home screen is depicted here).

APPLICATION	DEVICE	BASIC FUNCTION
Music	iPod touch	Enables the iPod functionality of your iPod touch, which allows you to listen to your music and podcasts.
Videos	iPod touch	Allows you to watch movies and other video, including those you may rent from iTunes.
Photos	Both	View photos that you have saved on your device. You can also use the photos as wallpaper, e-mail them, etc.
iTunes	Both	Browse the iTunes Music Store's vast catalog. You can preview before you buy, too.
App Store	Both	Discover applications, both paid and free, that you can download and use with your device.
Safari	Both	The default Web browser application for iPhone 3G/iPod touch.
Calendar	Both	Keep track of your appointments using this app. You can also synchronize Calendar with other calendar apps on your computer.
Mail	Both	Send and receive e-mail.
Contacts	Both	Store information about all of your contacts and sync them with your computer.
YouTube	Both	View any video in YouTube's gigantic collection from anywhere. Author: Literally any video, or the ones that have been converted to iPhone format? Tech
Stocks	Both	Allows you to keep up with the highs and lows of the stock market, anywhere and anytime.
Maps	Both	Never get lost again! This app helps you find your way, even providing driving directions should you need them.
Weather	Both	Stay abreast of the weather conditions and forecasts for any location.
Clock	Both	A one-stop timepiece shop, Clock lets you set alarms, contains a stopwatch and timer, and tells you what time it is anywhere in the world.
Calculator	Both	Perform simple calculations, or rotate the device sideways to use the advanced scientific functions.
Notes	Both	Take down notes anytime an idea pops in your head. You can also e-mail the notes to yourself or others.
Settings	Both	Configure your device's settings to customize its behavior. This app is covered in detail in Chapter 10.
Nike + iPod	iPod touch and iPhone 3GS	This app works in conjunction with certain Nike shoes to help you keep tabs of your performance during workouts.
Phone	iPhone	Provides immediate access to the phone features of your iPhone. You can make and receive calls, check voice mail, add and edit contacts, and more.
iPod	iPhone	Listen to music and podcasts, and watch your movies.
Messages	iPhone	Allows you to send and receive Short Message Service (SMS) text messages from your iPhone.
Camera	iPhone	Take pictures and record videos (iPhone 3GS only) using the built-in camera.
Voice Memos	Both	Record voice memos for yourself that you can play on your device, email to someone, or sync to your computer.
Compass	iPhone 3GS	Use the compass to determine your direction and to get coordinates for your current location.

Table 1-2: *Standard Applications with the iPhone 3G and iPod touch*

UICKSTEPS

USING MULTIPLE HOME SCREENS

Apple was brilliant enough to understand that you would want to install tons of additional applications on your new iPhone 3G or iPod touch but that there just isn't enough real estate on the default Home screen to add more than a handful. The answer to this dilemma is multiple Home screens. You can have as many as nine Home screens, each one containing as many as 16 application icons. After I broke out my calculator, I was able to determine that this means you can have as many as 148 applications (counting the 4 applications in the Dock) installed on your device. Using multiple Home screens is a breeze.

NAVIGATE BETWEEN SCREENS

There are a series of small dots near the bottom of your screen, but just above the Dock. These dots represent the number of Home screens you have and which one you are currently viewing.

- Flick the screen to the left or right to move between screens. You can also touch the dots to jump between screens.

- Press the **Home** button to return to the original Home screen from another Home screen.

CREATE A NEW HOME SCREEN

1. Press and hold an app icon until they all begin to wiggle.

2. Drag an icon to the right edge of the screen.

3. After a brief moment, the icon will jump over to a new Home screen, which you drop the icon onto.

Utilize the Home Button

You can hardly miss the Home button, especially since it's the only button on the front of your device. It's such an oft-used button that I've frequently wondered how many presses it takes to wear it out! So far, in my experience, it seems to be quite the stalwart.

The primary function of the Home button is to whisk you back to the Home screen from wherever you may be on your device. Pressing the Home button when using an application will close the application and put you back in the previous Home screen. However, the Home button isn't a one-trick pony; it can be utilized in conjunction with other buttons to perform some other important tasks.

- Force misbehaving applications to quit by pressing and holding the **Home** button down for at least six seconds.

- Reset the device by pressing and holding the **Sleep/Wake** and **Home** buttons simultaneously for 10 seconds, until the Apple logo appears on the screen.

- Take a picture of your device's screen by quickly pressing the **Sleep/Wake** and **Home** buttons simultaneously. The screen will flash when the picture is taken, and the picture can be found by pressing the **Photos** application icon and browsing your pictures.

The Home button performs other functions, but they pertain to using other applications, so I'll discuss those when warranted.

Navigate with the Touchscreen

The touchscreen on the iPhone 3G and iPod touch is one of the coolest features of any device on the planet. The first time someone experiences the ease with which you can maneuver using the touchscreen, they are almost instantly hooked. The movements are natural, so you'll quickly pick up on the nuances of moving around within the Home screen and in applications. Here's a quick tutorial on traversing the touchscreen's terrain.

- To open an application, simply touch its icon on the Home screen.

- To scroll up and down, place your finger on the screen and drag it up or down the screen, depending on the direction you want to scroll. Scroll to the right or left in

 UICK**STEPS**

DOUBLE-CLICK THE HOME BUTTON

You can double-click the **Home** button on your iPhone 3G to go quickly to the Home screen, your Phone Favorites, or to open the iPod functions.

1. From the Home screen, press **Settings**.

2. Choose **General**.

3. Touch the **Home Button** menu.

4. Select one of the double-click options provided.

5. Press the **Home** button to exit Settings and retain your choice.

TIP

To scroll quickly to the top of a list or Web page, tap the **Status** bar at the top of the screen.

the same manner. Scroll quickly through your list of contacts, for example, by placing your finger on the screen and flicking it in the desired direction to zip through the items on the screen. To stop the motion, tap the screen once.

- To select an item in an application, simply tap it. Many applications provide onscreen buttons, which you will also tap to invoke their functions.

- Zoom in and out of pictures, e-mails, web pages, or maps with incredible ease.

  - Zoom in by touching your thumb and forefinger together and placing them on the touchscreen. Begin spreading the thumb and forefinger apart while still touching the screen. How cool is that?

  - Zoom out by performing the action in reverse. Place your thumb and forefinger an inch or so apart on the screen, and pinch them together while still touching the screen.

  - Instantly zoom in on pictures and web pages by double-tapping (rapidly tapping twice) the screen. Zoom out by double-tapping again.

  - Zoom in on maps by double-tapping, but zoom out again with just a single tap.

Use the Onscreen Keyboard

Some applications, such as Mail and Safari, require the use of a keyboard. In case this little tidbit hasn't struck you yet, your iPhone 3G and iPod touch are keyboard-challenged, at least at first glance. However, your device has a hidden gem known as the onscreen keyboard (Figure 1-9), which utilizes the touchscreen technology to provide full keyboard functionality.

Figure 1-9: *The onscreen keyboard provides all the keys you will need for entering text, numbers, and other common characters.*

1. Tap a text field to open the onscreen keyboard.

2. To enter characters, simply touch and release, or tap, the appropriate key on the keyboard. When you touch a key, the character will appear above your finger; this helps you verify that you're pressing the intended key. If the letter that appears is not the one you intended, don't remove your finger from the screen; just slide your finger to the correct key and then release it to enter the character.

Shift key

Figure 1-10: The SHIFT key lights up when it's active.

Figure 1-11: The SHIFT key turns blue when caps lock is on.

Since the screen space is somewhat limited, certain conventions are necessary to approximate many of the functions of a standard keyboard.

● To enter a capital letter, tap the **SHIFT** key (Figure 1-10), and then tap the desired letter key.

● Turn on caps lock by double-tapping the **SHIFT** key. The key appears blue, as in Figure 1-11, when caps lock is on. If caps lock isn't working for you, enable it by tapping the **Settings** icon, selecting **General**, choosing **Keyboard**, and then tapping the **On/Off** switch to On for the Enable Caps Lock option.

● Press the **Number** key (contains ".?123" characters) in the lower-left corner of the onscreen keyboard to see the numbers and other characters, such as parentheses and quotation marks (Figure 1-12).

● When viewing the number keys, you can access other symbols (Figure 1-13) by tapping the **Symbol** key (contains the "#+=" characters) in the lower-left corner.

*Figure 1-12: **Numbers and other characters are also available on the onscreen keyboard.***

*Figure 1-13: **Access common symbols by tapping the Symbol button.***

● To get back to the letter keys from the numbers or symbols, simply tap the **ABC** key in the lower-left corner of the onscreen keyboard (Figure 1-14).

*Figure 1-14: **Get back to basics with the ABC key.***

QUICKSTEPS

CUSTOMIZING ICONS IN THE DOCK

Icons that reside in the Dock are always available, regardless of which Home screen you are on. You can customize the Dock so that it contains the apps you use most often.

1. Press and hold any app icon until they all begin to wiggle.

2. Drag-and-drop the icon of an app that you don't often use from the Dock and into the Home screen to make room for a new icon (there can be no more than four in the Dock).

3. Drag-and-drop the icon for the app you want to stay in the Dock from its location on the Home screen into the Dock.

- Sometimes you may want to use characters with your letters that you can't see on the keyboard, such as "é" for example. To view and select these characters, press and hold the desired letter key and then slide your finger to the character you want to use with it (Figure 1-15).

Arrange Icons

The applications you have on your device are represented by icons, which are typically descriptive of the function the app performs. For example, the icon for the Phone app is a green square containing (drum roll, please) a white telephone. These icons can be arranged in any order you like and can even be deleted.

*Figure 1-15: **Using nonstandard characters with your letters is simple.***

The icons are locked into position to prevent you from accidentally rearranging or deleting them. To unlock the icons, press and hold any one of them until they all begin to wiggle frantically, as if your phone was a Jell-O mold (Figure 1-16).

*Figure 1-16: **Your icons will wiggle when unlocked; they simply appear out of kilter in this shot.***

QUICKSTEPS

RESETTING THE DEFAULT ICONS

You may decide at some point that you like the applications you've added to your device, but you would like to have the default icons reset to their original locations on the Home screen.

1. Tap the **Settings** icon on the main Home screen.

2. Select **General**, and then choose **Reset**.

3. Tap **Reset Home Screen Layout**.

4. You will be prompted to confirm this action. Tap the **Reset Home Screen** button to commence with the reset.

5. Press the **Home** button to get back to your Home screen, which should be as good as new.

Once the icons are wiggling, you can either rearrange your icons or delete them (which uninstalls the app from your device).

- To rearrange the icons, drag-and-drop them to another location on the Home screen. As you drag an icon, the other icons instinctively move out of the way to make room for it. If you want a particular icon to reside on a different Home screen, drag its icon to the right or left edge of its current Home screen, wait for the Home screens to change, and then drop it onto the new Home screen.

- You can only delete icons for applications that you have added to your device; you cannot delete the default applications that came with it. To delete such icons, tap the **X** located in the upper-left corner of an icon. You will prompted to confirm this actions, as shown in Figure 1-17, so that your device can be sure you really do intend to delete the associated application.

- Press the **Home** button to stop the frantic wiggling of the app icons.

Figure 1-17: **Are you certain you want to delete an application?**

NOTE

You turn the volume up and down using the Volume buttons on the upper-left side of your device. The Volume buttons not only control the music volume, but also the volume of special effects, alarms, alerts, and the iPhone 3G's ringer.

Charge Your Device

Your device is just like any other in that it doesn't do much at all without being properly powered up. The iPhone 3G and iPod touch both contain rechargeable batteries, which will certainly run out of juice after a certain amount of usage. Your device came with a special USB cable meant for charging and syncing your device with a computer. One end of the cable connects to your device, and the other connects to a Universal Serial Bus (USB) port on your computer, or to the USB power adapter that also came with your device, which allows you to plug your device into an electrical outlet to reenergize itself.

1. You will be warned when the device's battery reaches a certain point, which is usually around the time the battery reaches 20 percent and 10 percent of its charge capacity.

2. Connect the device to a power source via its USB cable. A charge icon will appear in the upper-right corner. While the battery is charging, the icon will contain a lightning bolt.

3. Once the battery is charged to its full capacity, the charge icon in the upper-right corner will look like an electrical plug. If the phone is locked, press the **Home** button, and you will see a battery icon displayed with a full green gauge (Figure 1-18). You can disconnect the USB cable at this point; your device is completely charged.

Figure 1-18: **The battery is fully charged when the green gauge reaches all the way to the right.**

How to...

* Checking if iTunes Is Already Installed
* Register Your Device
* View Your Device in iTunes
* Understand the Summary Pane
* Preventing Automatic Syncing with All Devices
* Grasp the Info Pane
* Naming Your Device
* What Is MobileMe?
* Decipher the Ringtones Pane
* Understand the Music and Video Panes
* Creating Your Own Ringtones
* Use the Photos Pane
* Make Sense of the Podcasts Pane
* Grasp the Applications Pane
* Subscribing to Podcasts

Chapter 2
Configuring and Syncing Your Device with iTunes

Your iPhone 3G or iPod touch are great devices on their own, but they are even better when paired with Apple's iTunes application, which is available for both Mac and Windows-based PCs. iTunes is a nifty tool for managing your music, but when it comes to your iPhone 3G or iPod touch, synchronizing your media and other information is where it truly shines.

In this chapter, I'll show you how to get the latest version of iTunes, how to sync your device with your computer automatically and manually, and what options you can set to customize your synchronizations.

CHECKING IF iTUNES IS ALREADY INSTALLED

Think you may already have iTunes installed? Here's how to check your computer to see if iTunes is already on your system.

MAC

Look for the iTunes icon in your Dock at the bottom of your screen. The icon looks like a CD with a musical note superimposed on it.

–Or–

1. From within the Finder, press @ @**CMD+SHIFT+A** to automatically open a Finder window for your Applications folder.

2. Browse the list of applications for the iTunes icon.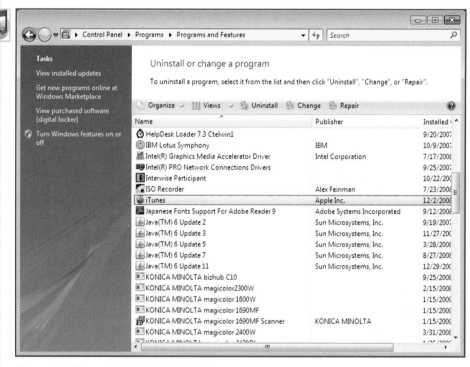

PC

1. Click the **Start** button in the lower-left corner of your screen.

2. Click **All Programs**.

3. Look for a folder called iTunes.

–Or–

1. Click the **Start** button.

2. Simply type iTunes and, if the application is installed, iTunes will appear in the Start menu.

–Or–

1. Click the **Start** button.

2. Click **Control Panel**.

3. Double-click **Add Or Remove Programs** (Windows XP) or choose **Programs** and select **Programs And Features** (Windows Vista).

4. Scroll through the list of installed applications and find iTunes (Figure 2-1).

Get iTunes

One of my favorite mantras is "First things first," and if you don't already have iTunes, you will need to get it before we proceed with the rest of this chapter. The chances are good that if you have a Mac, you already have iTunes installed. If you have a PC, those odds are reduced quite a bit, as it's not an item that's natively part of the Windows operating system.

1. Go to www.apple.com/itunes/download and click the **Download Now** button (Figure 2-2). You may need to choose an operating system version if you are on a Windows-based PC.

2. The download should begin at this point. Save the file to a location on your computer if prompted by your Web browser.

*Figure 2-1: **iTunes is installed on this PC.***

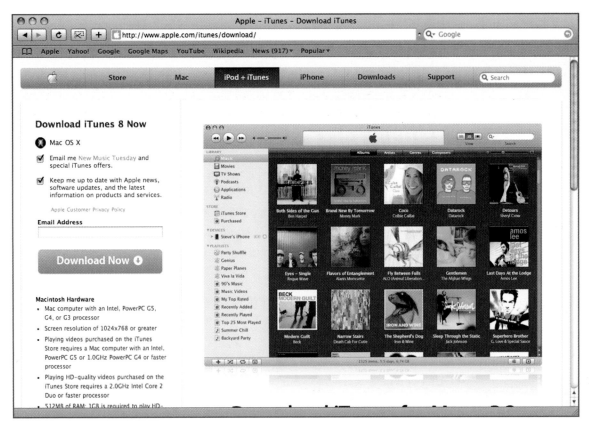

3. Some browsers may automatically run the installer file; others may not. If the installer doesn't begin as soon as the download is complete, browse to the location on your computer that the file was saved to.

● For Macs, double-click the **iTunes.dmg** file, and once the disk image mounts, double-click the **iTunes.mpkg** package. Follow the instructions to complete the installation.

● For PCs, double-click the **iTunesSetup.exe** file and follow the onscreen prompts to finish the installation.

4. Once iTunes is installed, you should launch it to verify the application opens properly.

Figure 2-2: *Click Download Now to download and install iTunes on your computer.*

NOTE

Be on the lookout for flashing User Account Control buttons in the taskbar if you're installing on Windows Vista. If you have User Account Control enabled on your PC, you will be prompted for permission to continue with the iTunes installation. Sometimes, those prompts can become hidden behind other windows. Click any flashing User Account Control buttons you may see in the taskbar to give your approval to install iTunes.

Synchronize Your Device

Synchronizing your device with iTunes will keep your information and media on both the computer and your device up-to-date. Did you add a contact to your iPhone today? Syncing will make sure the contact is also stored on your computer. Did you purchase a song in iTunes but want to listen to it on your iPod touch? Syncing will bring that song over into your device. iTunes will sync lots of stuff with your device.

- Applications downloaded from the iTunes Store
- Music
- Movies
- TV shows
- Audio books
- Podcasts

- Calendars
- Contacts
- Photos
- Web bookmarks
- Ringtones (iPhone 3G only)
- E-mail account settings

TIP

To avoid confusion and a myriad of other problems, you should be logged into your own user account on the computer with which you are syncing.

*Figure 2-3: **Your device will appear in the source list in iTunes.***

Register Your Device with iTunes

Registering your device with iTunes allows the computer to identify your device when it is connected. You must register before you can sync your iPhone 3G and before you can even begin to use your iPod touch.

1. Open iTunes.
2. Connect your device to your computer using the USB cable that came with it.
3. Follow the instructions provided by iTunes for registering your device.

View Your Device in iTunes

After you have registered your device with iTunes, you should see its icon in the left side of the iTunes window under the Devices section (Figure 2-3).

Set Sync Options

iTunes affords you the ability to automatically sync your device the instant you connect it to your computer, or you can choose to customize how iTunes syncs with the device. Several options can help you design your synchronizations to suit your needs.

Click the name of your iPhone 3G or iPod touch under the Devices section of the iTunes source list to see information about the device and access your synchronization options. There are several panes you can choose from when making settings selections, and these panes differ a bit between devices.

I will cover the settings panes for the iPhone 3G in the remainder of this chapter. I will mention which panes for the iPod touch correspond with similar functions on the iPhone.

Whenever you make a change to the settings in these panes, you must click the **Apply** button in the lower-right corner of the iTunes window to invoke the change, or click **Cancel** to revert to your previous settings.

Anytime you want to perform a synchronization of the items in these panes, click the **Sync** button in the lower-right corner of the iTunes window.

Understand the Summary Pane

The Summary pane (Figure 2-4) provides you with some important information about your device, including its name, memory capacity, the version of software currently installed, the serial number of device, and its phone number (if you have an iPhone).

*Figure 2-4: **The Summary pane is where you should start customizing your sync options.***

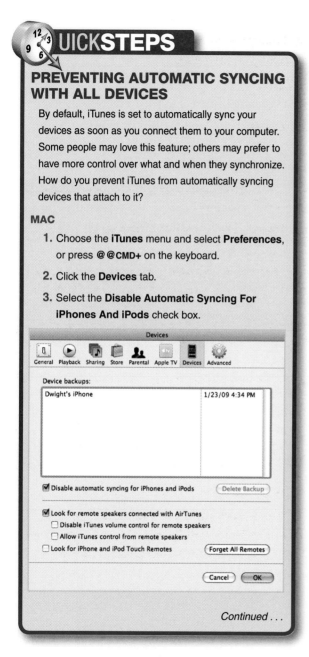

QUICKSTEPS

PREVENTING AUTOMATIC SYNCING WITH ALL DEVICES

By default, iTunes is set to automatically sync your devices as soon as you connect them to your computer. Some people may love this feature; others may prefer to have more control over what and when they synchronize. How do you prevent iTunes from automatically syncing devices that attach to it?

MAC

1. Choose the **iTunes** menu and select **Preferences**, or press **@ @ CMD+** on the keyboard.

2. Click the **Devices** tab.

3. Select the **Disable Automatic Syncing For iPhones And iPods** check box.

Continued . . .

OPTION	DEVICE	FUNCTION
Update	Both	iTunes will search Apple's servers for updates to your device's software. When it finds an update, you will be prompted to download and install the update file.
Restore	Both	You can restore your device to its original state by clicking the Restore button. You should only use this if you are experiencing serious problems with your device. Please see "Restore Your Device" for more information.
Automatically Sync When This iPhone Is Connected	iPhone only	You can enable or disable automatic syncing for this device only, as opposed to disabling auto syncing for all devices, by checking or unchecking this option.
Open iTunes When This iPod Is Connected	iPod touch only	Selecting this check box causes iTunes to automatically launch the moment your iPod touch is connected to your computer.
Sync Only Checked Songs And Videos	Both	iTunes places a check mark in the tiny boxes to the left of all of your songs and videos by default, which tells iTunes that these items can be synchronized with your devices. You can clear check boxes next to songs and videos in your iTunes Library that you don't want to sync with your device. Selecting this option will invoke this feature.
Manually Manage Music And Videos	Both	My favorite! This option puts you in control over adding and removing individual songs and videos. Please see "Manually Manage Songs and Videos," later in this chapter, for more info.

Table 2-1: Summary Pane Options for the iPhone 3G and iPod touch

Table 2-1 will explain the options found in the Summary pane of the iPhone 3G and iPod touch.

RESTORE YOUR DEVICE

iTunes makes a backup of your device's settings and information such as text messages, contact favorites, and the like when you connect the device

QUICKSTEPS

PREVENTING AUTOMATIC SYNCING WITH ALL DEVICES *(Continued)*

PC

1. Choose the **Edit** menu and select **Preferences**, or press **CTRL+** on the keyboard.

2. Click the **Devices** tab.

3. Select the **Disable Automatic Syncing For iPhones And iPods** check box.

CAUTION

It is extremely important to back up your device before restoring it! This will allow you to easily put your device back into the state it was in before restoring it (minus the problems that prompted the restore, of course).

to your computer. A restore will transfer your previous settings to your device and will replace the settings currently on the device.

1. Connect your device to your computer.

2. Open iTunes.

3. Select the device in the iTunes source list.

4. Choose the **Settings** pane.

5. Click the **Restore** button.

6. When prompted to back up your device, click the **Back Up** button. If you've just backed up your device, click **Don't Back Up**.

7. Click the **Restore** button when prompted to begin the restoration process.

8. Once the restoration is complete, your device will restart itself.

9. If you are restoring an iPhone, you must activate the phone with your cell carrier, so don't disconnect the phone during this process. You must have an Internet connection for this procedure.

10. iTunes will give you the option to set up your device as if it were new or to restore it using the backup you created earlier in this process. Select a backup from the pop-up menu, and click **Continue**.

11. After the restore is complete, you can disconnect the device.

MANUALLY MANAGE SONGS AND VIDEOS

If you selected the Manually Manage Music And Videos check box in the Summary pane, you now have the power to add individual songs and videos to and remove them from your device at your whim.

You can add videos, songs, entire playlists, and podcasts to your device.

1. Select the item or items you want to sync with your device. You can select multiple items by holding down the **SHIFT** or **COMMAND** (@@CMD) key while clicking each one.

2. Drag-and-drop the items onto your device's name in the iTunes source list.

3. The items are immediately synced with your device.

Figure 2-5: *When you drag an item to your device, it is instantly synced.*

You can also remove items from your device with equal ease.

1. Click the **gray triangle** to the left of your device's name to reveal its contents.

2. Find the item you want to remove.

3. Click the item and press the **DELETE** key on your computer's keyboard. The item will be removed from your device, but not from iTunes.

Grasp the Info Pane

The Info pane is a handy place to configure synchronization options for several types of information, in particular:

- Contacts
- Calendars

- E-mail accounts
- Web browser bookmarks

There are also two other important areas of this pane: MobileMe and Advanced. Let's take a look at each section of the Info pane so that you can get a handle on what the available options do for you.

MOBILEME

You can use MobileMe to sync items to your iPhone instead of using the other options in the Info pane, if you subscribe to the service.

CONTACTS

The Contacts section (Figure 2-6) of the Info pane lets you choose whether or how to sync the contacts on your computer with those in your device.

- Select the **Sync Address Book Contacts** check box (Mac) or the **Sync Contacts With** check box (PC) to have iTunes synchronize contacts on your computer with the Contacts app on your device.
- Decide whether to sync all contacts or only selected groups.
- Select the appropriate check box if you want to sync with Yahoo! Address Book or Google Contacts.

CALENDARS

Remembering those important dates and appointments can keep you out of hot water, and iTunes can help make sure that your calendars are synced on your computer and iPhone/iPod touch using the Calendars section of the Info pane (Figure 2-7).

- Select the **Sync iCal Calendars** check box (Mac) or the **Sync Calendars With** check box (PC) to enable calendar synchronization.
- Determine whether to sync all of your calendars or just certain ones.
- You can choose to not sync events older than a certain number of days.

MAIL ACCOUNTS

The Mail Accounts section lets you sync e-mail account settings between your computer and iPhone or iPod touch. This makes it simple to set up an e-mail

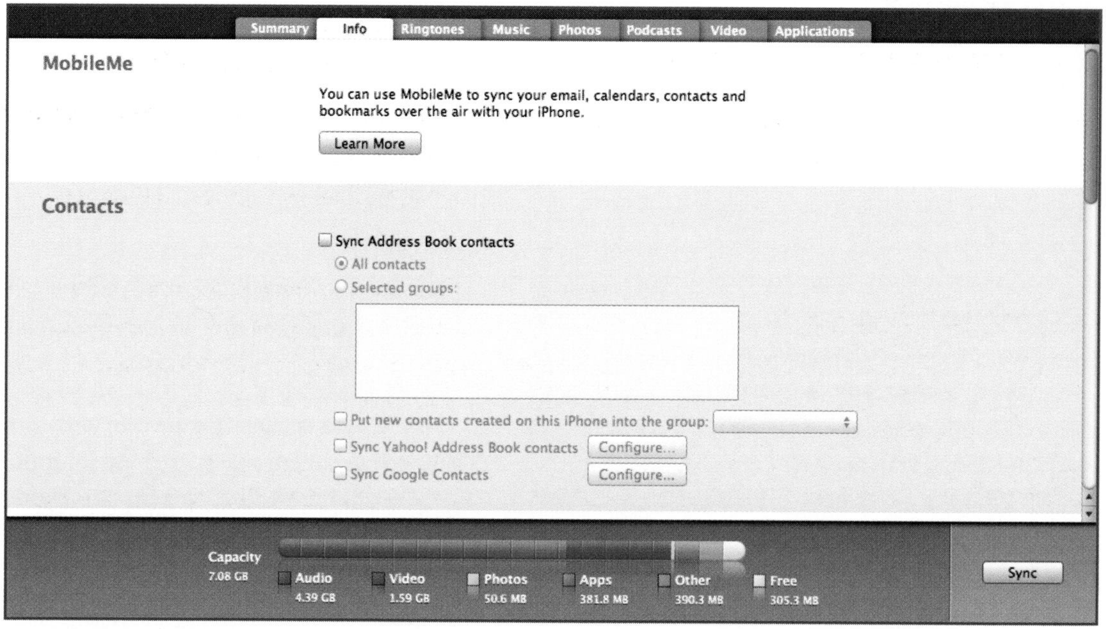

Figure 2-6: *Decide whether to sync your device's contacts with your computer.*

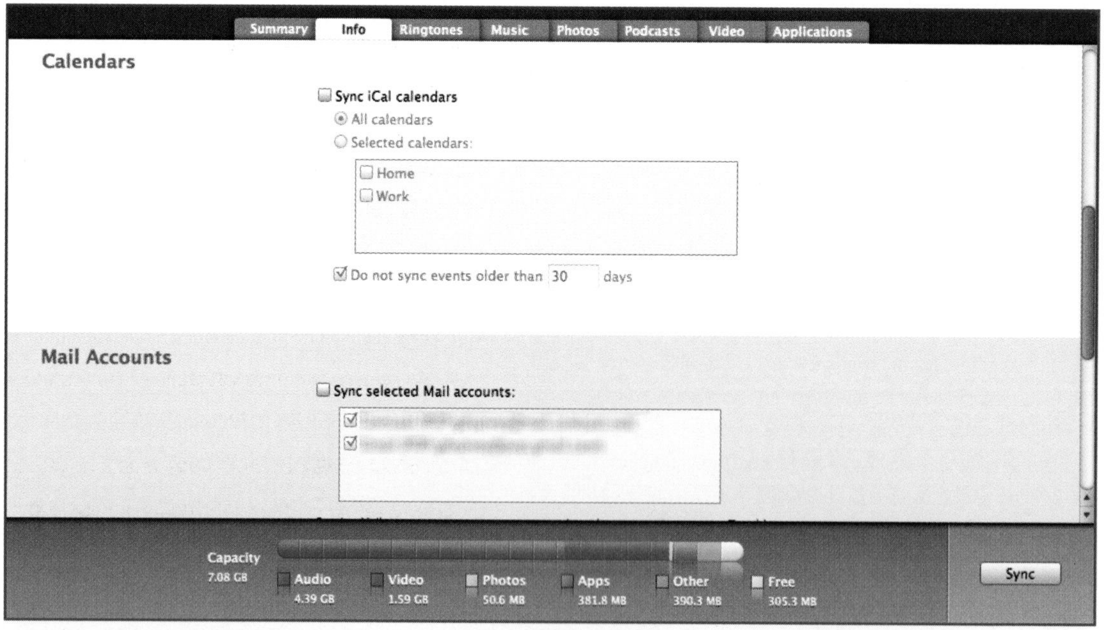

Figure 2-7: *Make sure you never forget that important date or appointment by syncing your calendars.*

NOTE

You can synchronize only the account settings, not actual e-mail messages.

NOTE

You can also synchronize Internet Explorer bookmarks if you use a PC, but you currently can't sync bookmarks with one of the Web's most popular browsers, Firefox (from either your Mac or PC).

account on your device, but you can also set up e-mail accounts manually (see Chapter 4 for more info).

1. Select the **Sync Selected Mail Accounts** check box.
2. Determine which e-mail accounts you want to sync your settings with.
3. Click the **Apply** button in the lower-right corner.

WEB BROWSER

Selecting the **Sync Safari Bookmarks** (Mac) or **Sync Bookmarks With** (PC) check box will allow you to synchronize the bookmarks you use in Safari on your Mac or PC with your device's Safari browser bookmarks. Explanations don't get much simpler than that!

ADVANCED

This section of the Info pane (Figure 2-8) can be both a blessing and a curse. You can choose to completely replace the contacts, calendars, e-mail accounts, and bookmarks of your device with those from your computer. In some cases, this can be a great thing, but if you accidentally invoke these tasks, you might be quite the unhappy camper. For example, if you've had to reinstall your computer's operating system, you will certainly not want to use this option, because these items on your device will revert to a blank slate if you don't have any contacts or other items on the computer yet.

1. Select the check box next to the type of information you want to replace.
2. Click **Apply**.
3. Click **Sync**.

Decipher the Ringtones Pane

Not too much going on here in terms of options (Figure 2-9), but it's cool to be able to synchronize your ringtones with your iPhone.

1. Select the **Sync Ringtones** check box to enable this feature.
2. Determine whether to sync all of your ringtones or only certain ones.
3. Click **Apply**, and then click **Sync**. That's all there is to it!

1 2 3 4 5 6 7 8 9 10

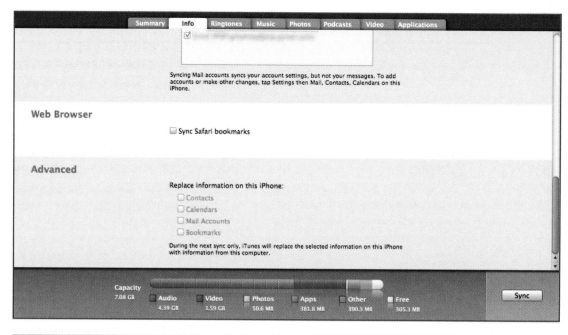

Figure 2-8: *The Web Browser and Advanced sections of the Info pane.*

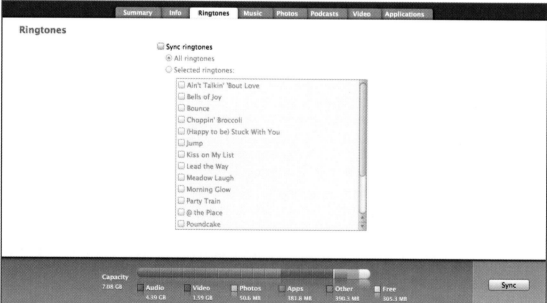

Figure 2-9: *Create your own ringtones and sync them with your iPhone.*

NOTE

The Movies and TV Shows panes on the iPod touch work
in the same manner as the Videos pane on the iPhone.

CAUTION

You can quickly run out of space on your iPhone or iPod
touch if you choose to synchronize your entire collection
of photos from your computer with your device. If you
have a large collection of photos on your computer, you
may want to sync only selected items.

Understand the Music and Videos Panes

The Music pane (Figure 2-10) and the Videos pane both help you easily
synchronize your music, TV shows, and movies. You can sync all the
songs and playlists in iTunes, or you can decide to sync only the playlists
you select.

1. Select the check boxes next to items you want to synchronize.

2. Click the desired option to sync all songs or just selected playlists, all episodes
of a television show; or select only certain movies you want to sync.

3. Click **Apply**, and then click **Sync**. Voilà! Your music and videos have been
synchronized.

*Figure 2-10: Can you tell by my music
playlists that I'm a child of the '80s?*

Figure 2-11: *Keep your photos in perfect sync using iTunes with your device.*

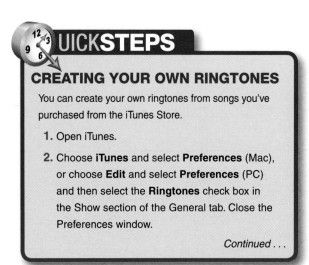

CREATING YOUR OWN RINGTONES

You can create your own ringtones from songs you've purchased from the iTunes Store.

1. Open iTunes.

2. Choose **iTunes** and select **Preferences** (Mac), or choose **Edit** and select **Preferences** (PC) and then select the **Ringtones** check box in the Show section of the General tab. Close the Preferences window.

Continued . . .

Use the Photos Pane

Syncing the photos on your device with your computer is a breeze using the Photos pane (Figure 2-11). You can sync photos with iPhoto 4.0.3 or later and with Aperture on your Mac, and with Adobe Photoshop Elements 3.0 or later and Adobe Photoshop Album 2.0 or later on a PC. You can also choose to sync photos contained within a certain folder on your computer.

1. Select the **Sync Photos From** check box.

2. Select an application or folder to sync with using the pop-up menu next to the Sync Photos From check box.

3. Decide whether to sync all photos or only select albums.

4. Click **Apply**, and then click **Sync**.

Make Sense of the Podcasts Pane

The Podcasts pane (Figure 2-12) is very much like the Music pane; this is where you go to choose how to synchronize podcasts that you've subscribed

to with your device so that you can listen to your favorites anywhere at any time.

1. Select the **Sync *X* Episodes Of** check box to enable podcast syncing.

2. Use the pop-up menu to choose how many podcasts to sync.

3. Determine if you want to sync all podcasts or only those you select from the available list.

4. Click **Apply**, and then click **Sync**.

Grasp the Applications Pane

Much like the other panes, the Applications pane (Figure 2-13) is a no-brainer. Whenever you download or purchase an application from the iTunes Store on your computer, as opposed to purchasing them from your iPhone or iPod touch, you must use the Applications pane to copy the app to your iPhone or iPod touch.

Figure 2-12: *Sync podcasts so that you stay up-to-date with their latest episodes.*

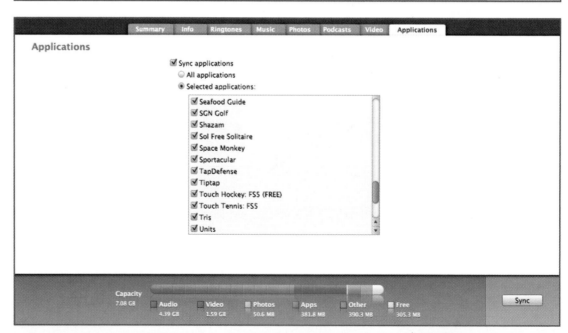

Figure 2-13: *Add and remove applications on your device using the Applications pane.*

QUICKSTEPS

SUBSCRIBING TO PODCASTS

Podcasts are essentially audio shows or videos that you can download from the Internet and listen to or view at your leisure using iTunes or your iPhone/iPod touch. When you subscribe to a podcast, iTunes will automatically download the newest episodes for you.

1. Click **Podcasts** in the source list on the left side of the iTunes window.

2. Click the **Podcast Directory** link near the bottom-right corner of the iTunes window, which will whisk you away to the Podcast section of the iTunes Store.

3. Browse the immense wealth of available podcasts until you find one that piques your interest, and click the **Subscribe** button. The most recent episode will automatically download to your computer.

4. Manage your podcasts by clicking **Podcasts** in the source list.

Also, when updates are released for the apps you have installed, iTunes will alert you and ask if it should download the updates; this pane helps you apply those updates when you perform a synchronization.

1. Select the **Sync Applications** check box.

2. Decide whether to update some or all of your apps.

3. Click **Apply**, and then click **Sync**.

CAUTION

Any apps you may have deleted from iTunes will also be deleted from your device when you synchronize them.

How to...

- *Make a Quick Call with the Keypad*
- *Use Contacts to Make a Call*
- *Receive a Call*
- *Using the Keypad During a Call*
- *Place a Call on Hold or Mute*
- *Use the Speaker*
- *Create New Contacts Manually*
- *Create a Contact from a Recent Call*
- *Utilize Favorites*
- *Assigning Ringtones to Contacts*
- *Silence Incoming Calls*
- *Handle Multiple Calls*
- *Utilize Visual Voicemail*
- *Changing Your Greeting*
- *Browse Recent Calls*
- *Use Other iPhone Applications During a Call*

Chapter 3

Making Calls with Your iPhone 3G

This chapter concentrates on the calling features of the iPhone 3G. The iPhone packs all the fun of the iPod touch into what is arguably one of the best cellular phones in the world. Apple took all of the features you would expect from a cell phone and made them more efficient, and even fun, to use. You can juggle multiple calls with unprecedented ease and use visual voicemail to listen to whatever message you want instead of having to listen to all of them. Adding contacts is a snap, and they've even thrown in such technical innovations as a keypad. Once you've made calls with an iPhone, it's nearly impossible to be satisfied with a more traditional cell phone.

Understand the Phone Buttons

Press the **Phone** application icon found on the left side of the Dock to initiate phone functionality for your iPhone. When the Phone application opens, you will see the five buttons at the bottom of the screen that will open the door to all of the features discussed in this chapter: Favorites, Recents, Contacts, Keypad, and Voicemail.

Table 3-1 offers a brief explanation of the treasures to be found within each of these important buttons.

Table 3-1: Basic Functions Contained in the Phone Applications Buttons

BUTTON	BASIC FUNCTIONS
Favorites	Quickly access your most frequently dialed contacts, whether they are family, friend, foe, or some combination thereof.
Recents	View the most recent calls you've received and/or missed.
Contacts	Browse through your list of contacts and easily add or edit contacts.
Keypad	Your basic everyday telephone keypad, but with a touchscreen instead of physical buttons.
Voicemail	Sort through voicemail with a flick of your finger and even listen to them in the order you choose instead of having to listen to several messages before getting to the one you want.

Use Basic Call Features

Some first-time iPhone users may be overwhelmed by what they perceive as a high-tech device instead of the amazingly user-friendly one designed by Apple. If you fall into that group, please let me quickly allay those fears. You won't find an easier cellular phone to use than the iPhone when it comes to making and receiving calls. Let's jump in with both feet and light up those cell towers.

Make a Quick Call with the Keypad

It doesn't get any more basic than placing a call to someone using the tried-and-true keypad, and iPhone makes this ancient technology almost seem new again with its touchscreen. To place a call with the keypad:

1. Touch the **Keypad** button at the bottom of the screen.
2. Enter the phone number you wish to call using the keypad buttons (Figure 3-1). Press the **Delete** button in the lower-right corner to correct mistakes.
3. Press the **Call** button to place your call.
4. iPhone takes you to the call screen, where you can view the status of your call (Figure 3-2).
5. Hang up the call by pressing the **End Call** button.

Figure 3-1: Touch the keypad buttons to enter a phone number.

Figure 3-2: You can see the status of your call on the touchscreen.

Use Contacts to Make a Call

Your contacts are records of the people you call the most, and they include all of the contact information for those people, such as multiple phone numbers or e-mail addresses. You can use these contacts to quickly call someone.

1. Press the **Contacts** button at the bottom of the screen.

2. Scroll through your list of contacts until you find the person you want to call, and then touch his or her contact.

3. When the contact information appears (Figure 3-3), touch the phone number at which you want to call him or her. iPhone will bring up the call screen, and away you go.

Figure 3-3: Simply touch a contact's number to initiate a call.

There's much more information on contacts later in this chapter, in the section called *Work with Contacts.*

Figure 3-4: An incoming call when the iPhone is locked

Figure 3-5: An incoming call when the iPhone is in use

Receive a Call

Chances are good that not only will you be making calls to folks, but those folks just might want to call you, too. You're in luck, because not only can your iPhone receive these calls, it can do it in style.

1. When you receive a call, your iPhone will, of course, ring (or vibrate if you've set it to silent mode; more on that later in this chapter). When the phone rings, the touchscreen will display the incoming call in one of two ways, depending on whether your iPhone is currently locked or in use. If the iPhone is locked, you will see a screen similar to that in Figure 3-4; if it's not locked, you will see something close to Figure 3-5.

2. To answer the call in locked mode, touch the **green arrow** at the bottom of the screen and slide it all the way to the right.

3. To answer the call when the iPhone is not locked, touch the **Answer** button.

4. Commence the conversation with a hearty "hello!"

Place a Call on Hold or Mute

If you need to take a break in the conversation for whatever reason, the iPhone gives you the option to put the call on mute or on hold. Placing the call on mute simply turns off the microphone of your iPhone so that the person you are talking to can no longer hear you but you can still hear him or her. Placing a call on hold will not allow either party to hear the other.

1. Hold the iPhone away from your ear to see the call screen.

2. Touch the **Mute** button to place the call on mute; the button turns blue to indicate that the call has been muted (Figure 3-6). Turn off mute by touching the Mute button again.

3. Touch the **Hold** button to place the call on hold; the button turns blue to show that the call is currently on hold (Figure 3-7). Take the call off hold by touching the Hold button again.

Figure 3-6: *Place the call on mute to keep the other caller from hearing you.*

Figure 3-7: *Place the call on hold, and neither caller can hear the other.*

Use the Speaker

Sometimes you need to use your iPhone hands-free, like when you're cooking dinner or chasing the kids. The iPhone has a surprisingly good speaker built in just for such occasions.

Figure 3-8: *The speakerphone is a convenient way to talk when you have to use your hands for other tasks.*

NOTE

Creating contacts on your computer goes much faster than on your iPhone. Be aware that any changes you create on the computer or iPhone will be copied to the other device during synchronization.

1. Hold the iPhone away from your ear to see the call screen.

2. Touch the **Speaker** button to initiate the speakerphone; the Speaker button turns blue to indicate that the speakerphone feature is in use (Figure 3-8). Turn off the speakerphone by touching the Speaker button again.

Work with Contacts

I briefly mentioned contacts earlier in this chapter, but we need to cover them in more depth now. Let's check out how to create new contacts, assign custom ringtones to differentiate your contacts, and use Favorites to make finding contacts easier.

Create New Contacts Manually

Contacts are added to your iPhone if you have synchronized it with a computer that you have contact information stored on, but you can also manually add contacts when you are away from your computer.

Figure 3-9: *The New Contact screen is waiting for your input.*

1. Touch the **Contacts** button at the bottom of the screen.

2. Tap the **+** button in the upper-right corner of the screen to open the New Contact screen (Figure 3-9).

3. Enter information about your new contact by tapping the appropriate field and using either the keyboard or keypad to type the data. After you have entered the desired information, press the **Save** button in the upper-right corner to return to the New Contact screen.

4. Press the **Save** button in the upper-right corner to save your new contact to the contacts list.

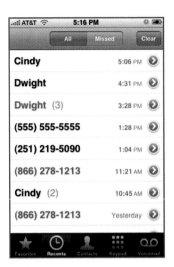

Figure 3-10: *Tap the Information button next to the number you want to make a new contact.*

Create a Contact from a Recent Call

Perhaps you just finished a call with someone who isn't in your contacts list, but you need to add them to it. No problem with the iPhone!

1. Touch the **Recents** button at the bottom of the screen.

2. Tap the **Information** button, which is the blue circle containing the arrow to the right of the phone number of the person you want to create a contact for (Figure 3-10).

3. Tap the **Create New Contact** button (Figure 3-11) to open the New Contact screen, where you can enter the appropriate information for your new contact.

4. Touch the **Save** button in the upper-right corner to add the new contact to your contacts list.

Utilize Favorites

The Favorites button at the bottom of the screen helps you to quickly find and contact the folks you converse with the most often. You can add, remove, or rearrange contacts to your Favorites list with ease (Figure 3-12).

To add a contact to Favorites:

1. Touch the **+** button in the upper-right corner.

2. Browse through the list of contacts, and tap the one you want to add. You may have to pick which phone number you want to add from the contact if there are multiples.

3. The contact is now in your Favorites list.

Figure 3-11: *Touch the Create New Contact button to add the contact's vital information.*

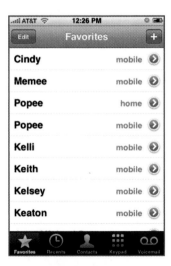

Figure 3-12: *The Favorites list helps find the contacts you use more often than others.*

NOTE

Contacts are removed from only the Favorites list during this process. The original contact information still resides in your Contacts app.

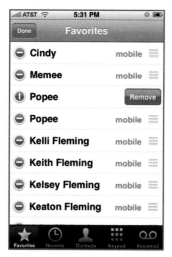

Figure 3-13: *Touch the Remove button to delete a contact from Favorites.*

To remove a contact from your Favorites:

1. Tap the **Edit** button in the upper-left corner of the screen.

2. Tap the **red circle** to the left of the contact you want to remove.

3. Tap the **Remove** button to the right of the contact (Figure 3-13), and the contact will be removed from the Favorites list.

4. Tap the **Done** button to return to the main Favorites screen.

To reorganize contacts in your Favorites:

1. Tap the **Edit** button in the upper-left corner of the screen.

2. Touch the **three horizontal bars** to the right of the contact, and drag-and-drop the contact into the desired position in the list (Figure 3-14). Other contacts will drop below or jump above the one you are moving as you drag it through the list.

3. Tap the **Done** button to return to the main Favorites screen.

Figure 3-14: *Drag the contact to a location in the list.*

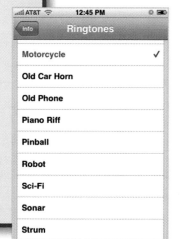

QUICKSTEPS

ASSIGNING RINGTONES TO CONTACTS

Distinguish who is calling you through nothing more than the ringtone by assigning a custom ringtone to a contact. See Chapter 2 for more on creating ringtones.

1. Touch the **Contacts** button at the bottom of the screen.

2. Select the contact you want to assign a custom ringtone to.

3. Tap the **Ringtone** button.

4. Choose a ringtone from the Ringtones screen by tapping the one you want to use.

Advanced Call Features

We've covered the basics of your iPhone's calling features, but there's much more to delve into that most users won't have to utilize on a daily basis. Let's look at how to silence incoming calls, juggle multiple calls at once, discover the wonders of visual voicemail, and even see how to use other iPhone applications while staying on a call.

Silence Incoming Calls

Doesn't it drive you crazy when you're sitting in a meeting or trying to enjoy a movie and the person in front of you is constantly getting calls on their cell phone and they don't even bother to silence the ring? Here are a couple of ways to make sure that you aren't the person everyone else is glaring at when someone inadvertently calls you in such a situation, or at least minimize your embarrassment.

- To completely silence all incoming calls, simply slide the **Ring/Silent** switch (found on the left side of your iPhone 3G) to Silent. When in Silent mode, you will see a red dot on the switch.

- To silence an individual call, press the **Sleep/Wake** button on the top of your iPhone. This will silence the ringtone, but the call will still come through normally.

Handle Multiple Calls

Busy people often find themselves jumping from one task to the next, and sometimes those tasks involve holding conversations with more than one person at a time. Or you simply may be on a call with a friend when your spouse calls you with news of the kids. Whatever the situation, dealing with multiple calls is something that most iPhone users will have to do at some point. Your iPhone can handle these situations with ease and elegance, as I'm about to illustrate.

ANSWER A SECOND CALL

So you're happily chatting away with someone when another friend decides to give you a call. What to do? Well, that decision is up to you. When the second call comes in, your iPhone will display the name or phone number of the calling party and give you three choices (Figure 3-15). Tap the appropriate button for the action you decide to take.

- Press the **Ignore** button to send the caller to your voicemail.

- Press the **Hold Call + Answer** button to place your current call on hold and answer the incoming call.

- Press the **End Call + Answer** button to terminate your current call and answer the incoming one. Don't forget to alert the person you're currently speaking with that you're ending the call, or they might not be too pleased with you.

SWITCH BETWEEN CALLS

Okay, you've just answered the second call, but you need to place the second caller on hold so you can return to the first caller. Never fear, iPhone is here!

Figure 3-15: **Decide what to do with a second incoming call.**

Figure 3-16: Tap the Swap button to jump back and forth between calls.

Figure 3-18: The call screen indicates when you are on a conference call.

Whenever you have multiple calls engaged, you will see them listed at the top of the call screen, as shown in Figure 3-16.

To switch between the calls, simply tap the **Swap** button. You can tell which call is on hold by looking to the right of the contact name near the top of the call screen.

CONFERENCE CALLS

Involve more than one person in your conversation by creating a conference call. Adding multiple callers to a conversation is easier than you might think.

1. While on a call, hold the iPhone away from your ear so you can view the call screen.

2. Tap the **Add Call** button, seen in Figure 3-17.

3. Select a contact to add to your conversation, or press the **Keypad** button in the lower-right corner to dial a number. The first call you were on is placed on hold while you call the other participant.

4. Tap the **Merge Calls** button to join the two calls together, creating your conference call.

5. The top of your call screen now indicates that you are on a conference call. To see the parties involved in the conversation, touch the circle containing the > in the upper-right corner of the call screen (Figure 3-18).

6. You have three options in the Conference screen (Figure 3-19):

   ● End one of the calls by touching the red circle with the white phone logo and then tapping the **End Call** button.

   ● Talk to one of the participants privately by touching the **Private** button.

   ● Go back to the main call screen by touching the **Back** button in the upper-left corner.

Figure 3-17: The Add Call button will help you make a second call.

Figure 3-19: You can easily manage your conference calls with iPhone.

Utilize Visual Voicemail

Visual voicemail is one of the coolest calling features on the iPhone. With visual voicemail, you can see the names or numbers of people who have called and left messages for you, and you can select any voicemail in the list to listen to it, instead of having to listen to all of your messages to get to the one you want to hear. Visual voicemail is a cinch to use, and you will love its convenience right from the outset.

The first time you touch the Voicemail button, your iPhone will prompt you to create a voicemail password and a greeting. You can choose to enter a password, or leave it blank if you prefer not to use one.

Here's how to use the features found in the visual voicemail screen:

- Unheard messages are displayed with a blue dot to the left of the contact name or number.
- Tap the blue button to the right of the contact name to see other pertinent information about the contact.
- There are a number of tasks you can perform when you touch the contact name or number in the message list.
  - Tap the **Play** button to the immediate left of the contact name or number to listen to the message. Tap the **Pause** button to temporarily stop the message; press **Play** again to resume.
  - Touch the **Call Back** button to return the person's call.
  - Touch the **Delete** button to remove the message. Deleted messages can be recovered by tapping the **Deleted Messages** option in the voicemail screen (if you don't see that option, you don't have any deleted messages).
  - Drag the **scrubber** while playing a voicemail to skip to another part of the message.
- The number of unheard messages is displayed in a small red circle on the Voicemail icon at the bottom of the screen.
- Tap the **Speaker** button in the upper-right corner to listen to a message using the iPhone's speakerphone feature.

CAUTION

If you choose not to use a password, your voicemail can be listened to by anyone who has access to your iPhone. If you don't want prying ears to know your business, a password is your best bet.

QUICKSTEPS

CHANGING YOUR GREETING

Don't care to use your cell carrier's standard voicemail greeting, or are you tired of the one you created the first time you set up visual voicemail? This is a malady that's simple enough to remedy.

1. Touch the **Phone** icon in the Dock.

2. Touch the **Voicemail** icon in the lower-right corner of the screen.

3. Tap the **Greeting** button in the upper-left corner to open the Greeting screen.

4. Tap **Default** to use your carrier's standard voicemail greeting.

5. Tap **Custom** to record your own greeting.

6. Touch the **Record** button to begin recording your new greeting. Press **Stop** to cease recording.

7. Touch **Play** to listen to your new greeting.

8. Tap the **Save** button when satisfied with your greeting.

Figure 3-20 shows a typical visual voicemail screen, along with its accompanying landmarks.

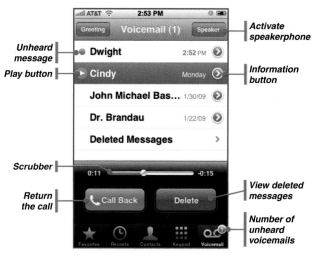

Figure 3-20: **You'll never want to go back to regular voicemail after using it on your iPhone.**

Browse Recent Calls

You can quickly view the most recent calls that you've made and received, including calls you may have missed. Touch the **Recents** button at the bottom of the screen to see a list of your recent calls (Figure 3-21).

A few tips for using the Recents screen are as follows:

- Calls you took are listed in black; missed calls are in red.
- Tap the **Information** button to the right of the contact name to view other information pertaining to the contact.
- Touch the **Missed** button at the top of the screen to only view calls you missed.
- Press the **Clear** button to wipe your Recents list clean.
- Touch the contact's name or number to call them.

Figure 3-21: *Check out your most recently made and missed calls.*

Use Other iPhone Applications During a Call

There may be times when you are on a call and you need to use other applications on your iPhone, such as Maps to find a location or Contacts to find a phone number for another friend. iPhone is able to handle this request with no problem.

1. Press the **Home** button while on a call to access the other applications on your iPhone.

2. iPhone places a green bar at the top of the screen that indicates you have an active call (Figure 3-22).

3. Use the other application you need.

4. When finished with the application, tap the green bar at the top of the screen to return to the active call.

Figure 3-22: *Touch the green bar to go back to your call.*

How to...

- Add an E-mail Account
- 🪐 Discovering Exchange Servers
- Configure Accounts
- 🎥 Configuring Your Account's SMTP Server
- 🎥 Removing an Account
- Utilize More Than One Account
- Check for New Mail
- See the Contents of E-mails
- 🎥 Setting the Number of Messages Shown
- View E-mail Attachments
- Delete E-mail
- 🎥 Deleting Multiple E-mails
- Move E-mail to Other Mailboxes or Folders
- Empty the Trash
- Reply to and Forward E-mails
- Create New E-mails
- 🎥 Adding a Signature to Outgoing E-mails
- Configure E-mail Fonts

Chapter 4
Communicating with Mail

E-mail has become as important a communication tool as the telephone for most of us, and has all but replaced the postal services for many, at least when it pertains to personal communications (sadly, most of us don't write letters anymore). Thanks to your iPhone or iPod touch, you will never have to be out of touch with your e-mail again when you are away from your computer. The Mail application on your device has made mobile e-mail so simple, yet deceptively powerful, allowing anyone from a busy mom to a businessperson to keep up with their electronic mail while on the go (and as always, to do it in style).

Setting Up E-mail

To use e-mail with your iPhone or iPod touch, you must first set up one or more e-mail accounts. iPhone and iPod touch support the most popular e-mail

Figure 4-1: Tap the button for your e-mail account type.

systems around, and you can set up the device to send and receive e-mail from them with little fuss or muss. Supported e-mail systems include:

- Microsoft Exchange
- MobileMe
- Gmail (Google e-mail)
- Yahoo! Mail
- America Online (AOL)

Add an E-mail Account

Adding an e-mail account is simple on your iPhone or iPod touch. Apple has instructed your device to configure settings automatically for the e-mail systems listed earlier, which makes setup a snap. E-mail systems other than those listed may need a little more configuration, but the work is still minimal.

1. From the Home screen, tap the **Settings** icon.
2. Touch the **Mail, Contacts, Calendars** button.
3. Tap the **Add Account** button.
4. If you have a Microsoft Exchange, MobileMe, Gmail, Yahoo! Mail, or AOL account, press the corresponding button. Select **Other** if you have a different POP3 or IMAP account (Figure 4-1).
5. Enter the information for your e-mail account, such as your name, e-mail address for the account, the password for the e-mail account, and a description of the account (such as Home, Work, School, etc.) by tapping a field and using the keyboard (Figure 4-2).
   - For Microsoft Exchange accounts, you will need to enter the domain name, your domain username, and your domain password. Contact your IT department for help with these settings, if necessary.
   - MobileMe and Microsoft Exchange accounts will be asked to select the items they want to synchronize.

Figure 4-2: Use the keyboard to enter your e-mail account information.

6. Tap the **Save** button.

7. Your device will verify your account information with your e-mail provider and create your account.

8. Press the **Home** button to finish the process.

Configure Accounts

Once you've added the e-mail account to your device, you are technically able to go ahead and jump into the Mail application, but to borrow a line from ESPN college football commentator Lee Corso, "Not so fast, my friend!" Everything may indeed be set correctly for your account, but I'm a big proponent of making sure before you continue. There may be a setting or two you want to adjust before diving right into your e-mail. You can access your e-mail account settings quickly.

1. From the Home screen, tap the **Settings** icon.

2. Tap the **Mail, Contacts, Calendars** button.

3. Touch the button for the account you want to configure.

DISCOVERING EXCHANGE SERVERS

Your device uses Microsoft's Autodiscovery service to find your network's Exchange server using your username and password information. If Autodiscovery cannot find your Exchange server, you will have to enter its address manually. You likely will need to contact your company's IT department to get the address, or they may even want to set up your Exchange e-mail on the device for you.

QUICKSTEPS

CONFIGURING YOUR ACCOUNT'S SMTP SERVER

If you are having trouble sending e-mail, you may have to make settings changes to your SMTP information. Check with your e-mail provider to see what settings they recommend before making changes on your own.

1. Open the **Settings** app and tap the **Mail, Contacts, Calendars** button.

2. Touch the account to which you want to make changes.

3. Tap the **SMTP** button under the Outgoing Mail Server heading.

4. Tap the button under the Primary Server heading.

5. Make any settings adjustments necessary, such as changing the host name, authentication method, or the server port.

Once you're here (Figure 4-3), you can check the configuration of your account.

- Enable or disable your e-mail account by touching the **On/Off** slider switch.

- You can change any account information as necessary, such as your account's password.

- Use the **SMTP** button to set the default Simple Mail Transfer Protocol (SMTP) server for this account. Leave at the default setting, unless your e-mail provider tells you to change it.

- Touch the **Advanced** button to see several more options for your account (Figure 4-4).

  - The **Mailbox Behaviors** section lets you decide whether to store draft messages and deleted messages in a mailbox on your device or on your e-mail provider's server. I suggest the latter, mainly for reasons of memory space.

- Adjust the **Incoming Settings** options only at the instruction of your e-mail provider.

Figure 4-3: Change just about any e-mail account behavior you need to from this screen.

Figure 4-4: The Advanced options screen of a typical e-mail account.

REMOVING AN ACCOUNT

Should you ever decide you no longer want to use an account on your device, you can remove its settings and accompanying e-mails.

1. Go to **Settings** and choose **Mail, Contacts, Calendars**.

2. Tap the account you want to remove under the Accounts heading.

3. Scroll to the bottom of the accounts screen and tap the **Delete Account** button.

4. When asked to confirm the removal, tap the **Delete Account** button again.

Utilize More Than One Account

If you have multiple e-mail accounts, you're in luck, because both the iPhone and iPod touch will let you use as many e-mail accounts as you need.

You will want to set your device's default e-mail account. This is so you can send e-mail from other applications in your device, for example, e-mailing a photo to someone.

1. Tap **Settings** on your device's Home screen.

2. Touch the **Mail, Contacts, Calendars** button.

3. Scroll down until you see the Default Account button, and then tap it.

4. Touch the button next to the account that you want to be your default (Figure 4-5).

When you open the Mail application, you can decide which of your accounts you would like to view.

1. Tap the **Mail** icon in the Dock (unless you've moved it from the Dock, of course).

2. Touch the name of the account you want to view in the Accounts screen (Figure 4-6).

Figure 4-5: Set your device's default e-mail account.

Figure 4-6: Which of your accounts would you like to view first?

Use Your E-mail Account

Now it's time for the fun part! Let's see how to use your e-mail accounts for the good of all mankind by learning how to see your e-mails and any attachments that may have hitched a ride on them, how to delete those e-mails you can no longer abide in your inbox, how to create new e-mails, and more.

Check for New Mail

There are three ways your device can retrieve new e-mails from your account's servers: pushing, fetching, or manually retrieving them.

Many account types, such as MobileMe and Microsoft Exchange, are considered push accounts, meaning that whenever new information arrives on the e-mail servers, that information is immediately sent to your iPhone or iPod touch.

For accounts that don't support push, you can use fetch, which tells your device how often it should check in with your e-mail servers to see if any new e-mail has arrived.

If you want to check for new e-mail at your convenience, or if battery life is getting low and you need to conserve, you will want to use the manual method.

1. Tap the **Settings** application on the Home screen and touch the **Mail**, **Contacts**, **Calendars** button.

2. Touch the **Fetch New Data** button.

3. Enable or disable push accounts by touching the **Push On/Off** switch.

4. If your account doesn't support push, select how often your device should search for new e-mail under the Fetch heading. Your choices are every 15 minutes, every 30 minutes, hourly, or manually (Figure 4-7).

5. Touch the **Advanced** button to choose a schedule for each account.

   ● Tap the name of the account you want to modify.

   ● Make a selection from the available choices (Figure 4-8).

Figure 4-7: To push or to fetch, that is the question (apologies to Mr. Shakespeare).

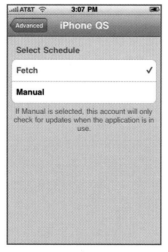

Figure 4-8: My iPhoneQS account is quite "fetching," indeed.

Figure 4-9: The number of unread e-mails is displayed in the little red circle on the Mail icon.

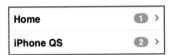

Figure 4-10: You can determine which account has unread e-mail by viewing the Accounts screen.

See the Contents of E-mails

I'm sure that by this point you're itching to actually see an e-mail, right? Assuming you have used all the correct settings for your account and that you do indeed have new e-mails in the account, you should have new e-mail on your iPhone or iPod touch by now. Whenever your device receives new e-mail, you can see the total number of unread e-mails in all of your accounts on the Mail icon (Figure 4-9).

Touch the **Mail** icon in the Dock to open the Mail application to the Accounts screen. If you have multiple accounts, you will see them listed here, and the number of unread e-mails contained in each will appear to the right of the account name (Figure 4-10).

1. Touch the name of the account whose e-mail you would like to view.

2. In the main screen for the account (Figure 4-11), you will see all the mailboxes for that account. Tap the mailbox (usually the inbox) that contains the e-mail you want to read.

3. You now see your list of e-mails (Figure 4-12). Beautiful, aren't they? Unread e-mail appears with a blue dot to its left.

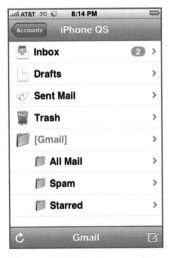

Figure 4-11: There are usually several mailboxes associated with an e-mail account.

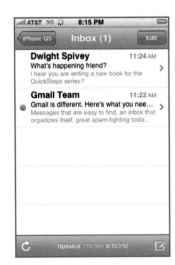

Figure 4-12: Scroll through your list of e-mails to find the one you want to read.

UICKSTEPS

SETTING THE NUMBER OF MESSAGES SHOWN

You can specify how many e-mails your device will display in the e-mail list. This comes in handy for e-mail accounts that you've had for a while and that contain hundreds of e-mails, all of which you probably don't want to download to your iPhone or iPod touch.

1. Tap the **Settings** icon on the Home screen.

2. Go to **Mail, Contacts, Calendars**.

3. Tap the **Show** button and choose to display 25, 50, 75, 100, or 200 of your most recent messages on your device.

4. Press the **Home** button after you've made your choice.

4. Tap the e-mail you want to view and—voilà!—there you have it (Figure 4-13). You can perform a plethora of actions from this screen. Let's take a peek at just a few; there's more information to come in this chapter about the items in the toolbar at the bottom of the screen.

- Tap **Hide/Details** in the upper-right corner to hide or show the To address.

- Tap **Mark Unread** to make the e-mail appear as if it's not been read yet in your e-mail list.

- Tap the **up** or **down** triangles in the upper-right corner to move to the previous or next e-mail in the list.

- Zoom in or out by double-tapping an area in the message.

- Manually resize a message by pinching two fingers together, placing them on the message, and (with both fingers touching the touchscreen) spreading them apart or pinching them together again. Is that cool or what?

- If there are links in your message (they appear as blue, underlined text), such as web links or phone numbers, just tap them to launch the appropriate application to handle whatever type of link it may be. To find out the destination of the link, touch and hold the link until the address is displayed.

Figure 4-13: A typical e-mail screen, proving that I do, indeed, have friends.

View E-mail Attachments

People send attachments in e-mails all the time, and your iPhone or iPod touch can display most attachments with ease. A paperclip icon will appear next to the e-mail sender's name in the e-mail list if there is an attachment included. Supported attachment file types are found in Table 4-1.

FILE TYPE	EXTENSION
Picture	jpeg, gif, tiff
Audio	mp3, aac, wav, aiff
Documents	txt, doc, docx, pages, pdf, htm, html, ppt, pptx, key, xls, xlsx, numbers, vcf

Table 4-1: File Formats Supported by the iPhone and iPod touch

Figure 4-14: Pictures typically show up in the body of the message.

Viewing attachments is quite simple.

1. Pictures sent as attachments generally appear inline with the message's text, as seen in Figure 4-14. To save picture attachments, touch the picture and tap the **Save Image** button (the picture will be saved in the Photo application).

2. Other attachments appear at the bottom of the e-mail message, illustrated in Figure 4-15, unless the sender placed the attachment somewhere else in the message.

3. To view an attached document, simply touch its icon in the message, and your device will open it (if it is a supported file type, of course), as shown in Figure 4-16.

4. To play an audio file, touch its icon, and the file will play over your device's speaker or headphones.

Figure 4-15: Scroll to the bottom of the e-mail to see the attachment, if necessary.

Figure 4-16: Attached documents are displayed right on your screen.

Delete E-mail

There are a couple of simple ways to delete individual e-mails when you no longer need them.

1. Open the e-mail.

2. Tap the **Trash** icon in the toolbar at the bottom of the screen (Figure 4-17).

Figure 4-17: When you tap the Trash button, the e-mail will appear to be sucked into it.

QUICKSTEPS

DELETING MULTIPLE E-MAILS

Deleting e-mail one at a time will get very tedious very quickly. There's an easier way to handle this situation.

1. Open the e-mail list.

2. Tap the **Edit** button in the upper-right corner.

3. Touch the radio button (circle) to the left of each e-mail you want to delete.

4. Press the **Delete** button in the lower-left corner to say goodbye to these unwanted e-mails.

Figure 4-19: Tap the Move icon to transfer an e-mail from one location to another.

NOTE

You can move multiple e-mails by tapping the **Edit** button, touching the radio buttons next to each message you want moved, and then tapping the **Move** button and selecting a folder to move them to.

– Or –

1. Viewing the e-mail list, quickly drag your finger across the ill-fated e-mail from left to right (or right to left, if that's more comfortable for you), and the Delete button will appear on the right side of the screen next to it (Figure 4-18).

2. Tap the **Delete** button to send that e-mail packing.

Move E-mail to Other Mailboxes or Folders

You can easily move e-mails from one mailbox or folder to another. An example of when you might want to do this would be if you accidentally deleted an e-mail and need to move it from the Trash mailbox back to your Inbox.

1. Open the mailbox or folder currently containing the e-mail.

2. Tap the e-mail to open it.

3. Tap the **Move** icon (Figure 4-19) in the toolbar at the bottom of the screen.

4. Select the mailbox or folder you want to move the e-mail to (Figure 4-20).

Empty the Trash

Every e-mail account on your device contains a Trash mailbox, which is where your deleted e-mail is stored until it's either automatically or manually removed on a permanent basis. You can empty the Trash at any time, as opposed to waiting for it to be done automatically in a few days.

1. Open Mail and enter the account you want to work with.

2. Touch the **Trash** mailbox to view the messages it contains.

Figure 4-18: Touch the Delete button to get rid of this e-mail.

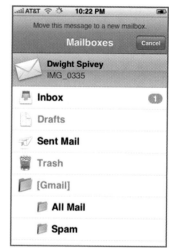

Figure 4-20: Find the mailbox or folder you want to move the e-mail to and tap it.

3. Tap the **Edit** button.

4. Delete all e-mails or only certain ones.

   ● Touch the radio button to the right of an e-mail or several e-mails to delete them individually, and then tap the **Delete** button in the lower-left corner.

   –Or–

   ● Touch the **Delete All** button in the lower-left corner, and then tap the **Delete All** confirmation button to remove instantly all the e-mails in your Trash.

Reply to and Forward E-mails

Replying to e-mails that others send to you, or forwarding those e-mails to other people, is simple enough with the iPhone and iPod touch.

1. Open the e-mail you want to reply to or forward.

2. Tap the **Reply/Forward** button in the toolbar at the bottom of the screen (Figure 4-21).

Figure 4-21: *Tap the Reply/ Forward icon to send the e-mail to someone else.*

3. Tap the **Reply**, **Reply All** (if sending to multiple recipients), or **Forward** button.

4. Tap the **To**, **Cc**, or **Bcc** fields to add addresses, if necessary, and then type the body of your message (Figure 4-22).

5. Tap the **Send** button in the upper-right corner when ready to deliver your e-mail.

Create New E-mails

At some point, you're certainly going to need to compose your own e-mails, so let's see how to go about doing so.

1. Open Mail and go into the e-mail account you want to send the e-mail from.

Figure 4-22: *Use the keyboard to type your addresses and message.*

QUICKSTEPS

ADDING A SIGNATURE TO OUTGOING E-MAILS

If you've ever received an e-mail from someone that uses an iPhone or iPod touch, you've probably noticed the words "Sent from my iPhone" at the bottom of the message. This is the default signature the Mail program uses for all messages it sends. You can customize that signature, typing in your own message or leaving it blank altogether.

1. Open **Settings**.

2. Tap the **Mail, Contacts, Calendars** button.

3. Touch the **Signature** button to open the Signature screen.

4. Press the **Clear** button in the upper-right corner if you want to start from scratch or want to leave the signature blank.

5. Enter your customized signature using the onscreen keyboard.

6. Tap the **Mail** button in the upper-left corner to exit the Signature screen, or press the **Home** button to jump back to the Home screen.

---

2. Tap the **New Mail** button in the lower-right corner (Figure 4-23). This button appears on other e-mail screens as well, for added convenience.

3. Enter the addresses you want to send the e-mail to (the list of contacts comes up automatically when you touch the To, Cc, or Bcc fields), as well as the subject and body of the e-mail, using the onscreen keyboard.

4. Tap the **Send** button in the upper-right corner to zip the e-mail along to its intended recipient.

Figure 4-23: The New Mail button will open a new e-mail for you to customize and deliver.

Configure E-mail Fonts

There's not a lot you can do when it comes to fonts on your device, but in Mail, you can at least control the default size.

1. Open **Settings** from the Home screen.

2. Tap the **Mail, Contacts, Calendars** button.

3. Select the **Minimum Font Size** button.

4. Choose **Small**, **Medium** (Figure 4-24), **Large**, **Extra Large**, or **Giant** (Figure 4-25).

5. Press the **Home** button to exit to the Home screen, or tap the **Mail** button to return to the Mail, Contacts, Calendars screen.

Figure 4-24: An e-mail composed with the Medium font size

Figure 4-25: An e-mail composed with the Giant font size

How to...

- *Understand Safari's Interface*
- *View Web Pages*
- *Using Specialized iPhone/iPod touch Web Sites*
- *Enter an Address in the URL Field*
- *Zooming In and Out of Pages*
- *Navigate Web Pages*
- *Closing a Web Page*
- *Handle Multiple Browser Pages*
- *Choose a Default Search Engine*
- *Create New Bookmarks*
- *Open a Site with a Bookmark*
- *Manage Your Bookmarks*
- *Editing Bookmarks*
- *Use the History List*
- *Clearing the History List*
- *Get the Latest News with RSS Feeds*
- *Save an Image to Your Device*
- *Calling Phone Numbers Listed on Web Pages*
- *Use Web Clips on the Home Screen*

Chapter 5

Surfing the Web with Safari

It seems that the Web is everywhere these days; there are wireless hotspots in just about every coffee shop and bookstore on the planet, not to mention the networks in offices and homes. In many larger cities, it's getting more difficult to find an area where you can't find an Internet connection. Your iPhone and iPod touch are ready to rock on the Web right out of the box. The iPod touch can use any wireless Internet system you have access to, and the iPhone can use both a wireless network and the 3G or Edge network of your cell phone carrier. You have the power of the Internet in the palm of your hand just about anywhere you go, and with Safari, the default web browser on your device, you will be surfing with a real browser, not some half-baked attempt at one, the likes of which are so prevalent on most cell phones.

URL field

Search field

Browser window

Next button

Previous button

Action button

Bookmarks button

Pages button

Figure 5-1: **The Safari screen is simple functionality at its best.**

Figure 5-2: **Apple's web site as seen in Safari on my iPhone 3G.**

Safari Basics

Let's get down to business by using Safari to cruise the Internet. In this section of the chapter, we'll see how to move around in Safari's interface, view and navigate web pages, juggle multiple web pages, and more. To get started, open Safari by tapping its icon (it looks like a compass) in the Dock.

Understand Safari's Interface

Safari's basic screen (Figure 5-1) may surprise you with its simplicity, but that simplicity is deceptive. As we go along, you will be amazed at how much of a full browsing experience Safari on your iPhone or iPod touch will give you. Table 5-1 gives you a brief explanation of the landmarks found on the Safari screen.

LANDMARK	FUNCTION
URL field	Displays the address of web pages. Enter new web addresses in this field, too.
Search field	Type in topics you wish to search on the Internet.
Browser window	Displays web pages.
Pages button	Allows you to manage multiple web pages.
Bookmarks button	View your bookmarks and history.
Action button	Lets you perform an action for a web address, like adding it to your bookmarks or e-mailing the link to a friend.
Previous button	Scroll backward in your list of viewed pages.
Next button	Scroll forward in your list of viewed pages.

Table 5-1: **Functionality of Buttons and Fields in Safari**

View Web Pages

Safari is unique among mobile web browsers in that it was the first, and is still easily the best, at giving you a true browsing experience. When you view a web page in Safari, you are seeing the entire page, just as you would see it on a Mac or PC's web browser. This is a feature not found in the vast majority of mobile web browsers, and even those that do supply this functionality don't perform nearly as well. Figure 5-2 shows how Apple's web site looks on my iPhone.

NOTE

Some web sites may be easier to read than others, depending on their content and layout. The less the page is cluttered and the larger the fonts, the better, of course.

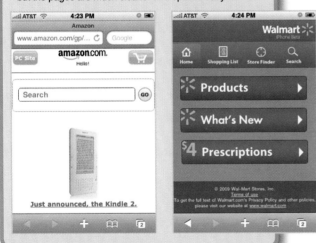

QUICKFACTS

USING SPECIALIZED iPHONE/iPOD TOUCH WEB SITES

A few web sites, such as Amazon.com and Walmart.com, are beginning to redirect iPhone and iPod touch Safari users to special sites specifically designed for use with mobile Safari. You can still access the information you seek, but the pages are much cleaner and options easy to find.

NOTE

Most addresses won't require you to enter "http://" or "www." when entering them, saving you significant amounts of typing.

As you can see in Figure 5-2, and on your iPhone or iPod touch as well, the web site is all there, but is a bit tiny for most eyes. You may be able to remedy this problem quite easily by simply turning your phone to landscape mode. The web page will flip over so that you can view it in a widescreen format (Figure 5-3).

Figure 5-3: **Landscape view can make looking at web sites even better.**

Enter an Address in the URL Field

You enter web addresses, or Uniform Resource Locators (URLs), into your device's Safari the same way you do with your computer: using the keyboard.

1. Tap the **URL** field to bring up the touchscreen's keyboard (Figure 5-4).

2. Use the keyboard to enter the name of the web site you want to visit.

3. Tap the **X** on the right side of the URL field to clear the field completely.

Figure 5-4: **Enter a character by tapping it on the keyboard.**

NOTE

There is a special key on Safari's keyboard called ".COM" that will append the .com extension onto the end of a URL for you, saving you a few keystrokes. Those few keystrokes can add up over time, so don't dismiss the .COM key out of hand; give it a shot.

QUICKSTEPS

ZOOMING IN AND OUT OF PAGES

Elements on web pages can look small, but Apple has figured out a cool way to get around that little snafu: zooming in and out. Move around the zoomed-in web page by dragging your finger over the touchscreen.

1. Pinch two fingers together (usually your thumb and forefinger) and place them on the touchscreen.

2. While still touching the screen, spread your fingers apart to zoom in on an area.

3. Zoom back out by placing your spread fingers back on the screen and then pinching them back together.

–Or–

1. Double-tap the area of a web page to zoom in on that area.

2. Double-tap again to zoom back out.

4. To edit your address, press and hold the **URL** field, and when the magnifying region opens (Figure 5-5), drag your finger to the point you want to edit.

*Figure 5-5: **Edit with ease using the magnifying glass.***

5. Tap the **Go** button in the lower-right corner of the keyboard to zoom to the site.

Navigate Web Pages

Once you have a Web page up, you will no doubt want to peruse its contents or choose links contained therein. This section is a quick primer on navigating elements within a typical web page.

- To go to a link on a page, simply tap the link.

- To see the address of a link, touch and hold the link, and the address will pop up (Figure 5-6). You also have options to open the page in the link, open the link in a new Safari page, or copy the link.

- To stop a page from loading, tap the **X** on the right side of the URL field.

- To reload a page, tap the **refresh** icon (looks like a circular arrow) on the right side of the URL field.

*Figure 5-6: **Touch and hold a link to see its destination address.***

NOTE

The Pages button in the lower-right corner of the screen will reflect the number of web pages you currently have open.

Figure 5-8: Scroll through your open pages with a flick of your finger.

- Tap the **Previous** button to go backward in the list of sites you've visited.
- Tap the **Next** button to go forward in the list of sites you've visited.

Handle Multiple Browser Pages

Most of us are used to having multiple web pages open at one time when using a browser on our computer, especially since the advent of tabbed browsing, which allows you to have multiple pages open within a single browser window. While Safari can't yet handle tabbed browsing, it can approximate it fairly well, as you can have several web pages loaded at any given time and can browse between them quite easily.

To open a new web page:

1. Tap the **Pages** button in the lower-right corner of the screen.

2. Tap the **New Page** button in the lower-left corner (Figure 5-7).

3. Enter the address of the new page in the URL field.

To browse between pages:

1. Tap the **Pages** button again in the lower-right corner.

2. Drag your finger on the screen to the left or right to scroll to the page you want to view (Figure 5-8).

3. Tap the **Done** button or tap the web page you want to view to open it on your screen.

Choose a Default Search Engine

Google is the default search engine for Safari, but you can easily change to Yahoo! should you prefer.

1. Tap the **Settings** button on the Home screen.

2. Scroll down the Settings screen and touch the **Safari** button.

3. Touch the **Search Engine** button.

Figure 5-7: Tap New Page to open a new web site.

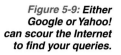

*Figure 5-9: **Either Google or Yahoo! can scour the Internet to find your queries.***

4. Tap either **Google** or **Yahoo!** to set up one as the default search engine (Figure 5-9).

5. Press the **Home** button when finished.

Utilize Bookmarks

If you are familiar with browsing on your computer, you probably understand how to use bookmarks. Bookmarks are links to web pages that you visit often, and using them can prevent you from having to repeatedly type in the addresses each time you go to visit those pages. While the touchscreen keyboard on your iPhone or iPod touch is surprisingly easy to use, it's still not as easy as a conventional computer keyboard, so the benefits of using bookmarks on these devices should be self-evident. By the same token, it's also easier to create bookmarks and organize them using your computer and then synchronize them with your device.

Create New Bookmarks

The first step to using bookmarks is to actually create one, so let's get started.

1. Open a web page that you visit often.

2. Tap the **Action** button at the bottom of the screen (looks like a +).

3. Tap the **Add Bookmark** button when it appears (Figure 5-10).

4. Edit the information in the Add Bookmark screen if you need to (Figure 5-11).

5. Select a folder to save the bookmark in, or just leave it at the default folder if you wish.

6. Tap the **Save** button in the upper-right corner to save the bookmark to the specified folder.

*Figure 5-10: **Tap the Add Bookmark button to create a bookmark for the site you're viewing.***

*Figure 5-11: **Change the name of the bookmark if you wish, or edit its address.***

Figure 5-12: *Your bookmarks will be listed on this screen or in one of the available folders.*

Open a Site with a Bookmark

Now that you have some bookmarks of your own, let's see how to open a web page using them.

1. Tap the **Bookmarks** button (it looks like an open book) at the bottom of the screen.

2. In the Bookmarks screen (Figure 5-12), find the bookmark for the site you want to open and then tap it.

3. Safari opens the site in the current page. Create a new page if you don't want to open the new site in place of one you were already viewing.

Manage Your Bookmarks

Your list of bookmarks can get quite lengthy, so you'll want to periodically go through them, possibly deleting some or putting them into folders. You can even rearrange their placement in the bookmarks list, moving your favorites to the top for easier access.

To get started, tap the **Bookmarks** button to open the Bookmarks screen, tap the **Edit** button in the lower-left corner, and then perform one of the following tasks:

- Delete a bookmark or folder by tapping the red circle to the left of its name and then tapping the **Delete** button to its right.

NOTE

Your device comes with a few predefined bookmarks, such as links to the device's user guide or your cell carrier's account information.

EDITING BOOKMARKS

Sometimes, the address of a bookmarked site may change, or you might want to change the title of the bookmark to something more descriptive. Those are easy enough tasks to perform with your iPhone or iPod touch.

1. Tap the **Bookmarks** button at the bottom of the screen.

2. Tap the **Edit** button in the lower-left corner.

3. Touch the name of the bookmark you want to edit.

4. Make changes to the information in the Edit Bookmark screen as needed, and then tap the **Bookmarks** button to go back to the Bookmarks screen.

- Rearrange a bookmark's position in the list by touching the three horizontal bars to the right of the bookmark and dragging-and-dropping it into the new position.

- Create a new folder by tapping the **New Folder** button in the lower-right corner. Enter a title for the folder in the Edit Folder window, choose a location for it, and then tap the **Bookmarks** button in the upper-left corner of the screen. Your new folder will appear in the list.

Use the History List

Have you ever closed a web site, wanted to go back to it, but couldn't remember its URL? The History list on your iPhone or iPod touch can help you locate the lost site and reopen it in a flash.

1. Touch the **Bookmarks** button at the bottom of Safari's screen.

2. Tap the **History** folder.

3. Browse the list or folders of previous dates to find the site you want to view.

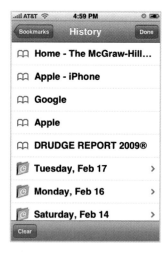

4. Tap the name of the site, and Safari will open it right up.

QUICKSTEPS

CLEARING THE HISTORY LIST

Your History list can get a little crowded after a while, but luckily, you can clear it out and start over.

1. Tap the **Settings** button on the Home screen.

2. Scroll until you see the Safari button, and then tap it.

3. Touch the **Clear History** button, and then tap the **Clear History** button again when prompted.

NOTE

You can download Safari for Mac or Windows by visiting www.apple.com/safari.

TIP

Organize your RSS bookmarks by creating an RSS folder. That way, it will be easier to differentiate RSS feeds from regular web sites in your Bookmarks screen.

Advanced Safari

Safari can do a few things that might surprise you, and they go beyond the bare basics of web browsing; hence, I consider them to be advanced. Stay up-to-date on late-breaking news with Really Simple Syndication (RSS), save images from the Web directly to your iPhone or iPod touch, and even launch web pages straight from your Home screen as if they were applications.

Get the Latest News with RSS Feeds

Safari can help you keep up with late-breaking news from your favorite web sites using RSS, but it will require the use of Safari on your Mac or PC.

1. Open a favorite site in Safari.

2. If the site supports RSS feeds, you will see an RSS icon in the right side of the URL field (Figure 5-13). Click the **RSS** icon to open the RSS feed page for the site.

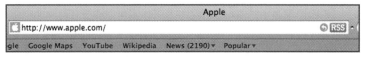

Figure 5-13: The blue RSS icon indicates that the site you are viewing supports an RSS feed.

3. Bookmark the RSS feed page, being certain to select the Safari check box as opposed to the Mail check box.

4. Connect your device to your computer and open iTunes.

5. Select the device in the source's list of iTunes, and then click the **Info** tab.

6. Select the **Sync Safari Bookmarks** check box in the Web Browser section, and click the **Sync** button in the lower-right corner to synchronize bookmarks with your iPhone or iPod touch.

7. Open Safari on your device and tap the **Bookmarks** button at the bottom of the screen.

8. The RSS feed will appear in your bookmarks list: Tap the feed to open it in Safari (Figure 5-14).

Figure 5-14: The latest news is always at your fingertips with RSS.

Save an Image to Your Device

You're surfing the Web on your iPhone or iPod touch and find a picture that you just have to keep for viewing later or sharing with others. This is an easy task for Safari.

1. Press and hold the image you want to save until the Task menu (Figure 5-15) pops up.

Figure 5-15: Save the image, open or copy its link, or cancel the operation altogether.

2. Touch the **Save Image** button. This saves the image to your Camera Roll (iPhone) or Photo Library (iPod touch).

3. To view the image, go to the Home screen and tap the **Photos** app. If your device is an iPhone, the image can be found in your Camera Roll; if you have an iPod touch, the image is in your Photo Library.

Use Web Clips on the Home Screen

Web clips are essentially quick links to your favorite web sites. Web clips reside on your Home screen just like your applications. When you touch a web clip on the Home screen, Safari automatically launches the web site; as a matter of fact,

---

CALLING PHONE NUMBERS LISTED ON WEB PAGES

A cool feature of Safari is that you can click a phone number on a web page, and Safari automatically launches the Phone app on your iPhone and the number is called. Now that's what I call convenient!

1. Locate a phone number on the web site you have open. The phone number will appear as a blue link.

2. Tap the phone number.

3. iPhone asks if you want to call the number or cancel. Tap the **Call** button to make the call.

Figure 5-16: *The Task menu lets you decide what to do with the current web page.*

it opens to the exact spot on the page that you were viewing when you created the web clip.

1. Open a site you want to create a web clip for.
2. Tap the **+** button at the bottom of the screen to open the Task menu (Figure 5-16).
3. Touch the **Add To Home Screen** button.
4. Edit the name of the web clip in the Add To Home screen if you like (Figure 5-17).
5. Tap the **Add** button in the upper-right corner to put an icon for the web clip on your Home screen.

Figure 5-17: *Give your web clip a descriptive name to help you remember what it is.*

How to...

- *Learning More About iTunes*
- Understand the iTunes Interface
- Import Audio into iTunes
- *Viewing Your Library with Cover Flow*
- *Adding Lyrics to Your Songs*
- Check Out the iTunes Store
- Subscribe to Podcasts
- *Continuing Your Education with iTunes U*
- Sync Music with iTunes
- Create Playlists
- *Turning On Genius Playlists*
- Create Smart Playlists
- *Copying Playlists to Your Device*
- Format Movies for the iPhone/iPod touch with iTunes
- Rent or Buy Movies from the iTunes Store
- Sync Video with iTunes
- Browse Playlists, Artists, and Songs
- Organize Albums, Audiobooks, Compilations, Composers, Genres, and Podcasts
- *Downloading Podcasts with Your iPhone 3G/iPod touch*
- Understand the Playback Controls
- Browse Your Music with Cover Flow
- *Configuring the Toolbar*
- Watch Video on Your iPhone 3G/ iPod touch

Chapter 6

Enjoying Music and Video

An iPhone or iPod touch without music or video is like a math nerd without a scientific calculator: it doesn't compute. Listening to your favorite music or audio files and watching video, in the palm of your hand wherever you may go, are two of the primary reasons for having one of these devices in the first place. Both devices would be functional without these digital mediums, but like breakfast cereal without the milk, something major wouldn't be quite right.

Using iTunes

iTunes is the primary gateway for your device to communicate with your computer, which is where you will have most of your music and video stored.

Using iTunes, you can synchronize your tunes and vids, as mentioned in Chapter 1, but you can also do much more.

- Create playlists of your favorite audio files.
- Rent and buy movies.
- Organize your audio and video library.
- Create ringtones for your iPhone.
- Burn audio CDs.

Understand the iTunes Interface

The iTunes interface is easy to get around in, but there are certain landmarks that bear explanation. Figure 6-1 gives you the lay of the land, and Table 6-1 gives a brief explanation of the major elements.

ITEM	FUNCTIONS
Search	Enter any information about the item you are trying to find, and iTunes will display all of the corresponding items. The more information you enter, the more you can narrow down the search.
Status window	See the name of the track currently playing, as well as the amount of time that has elapsed and is still remaining.
Track list	Displays the items in your library, allowing you to arrange them according to the column headings. Click a column heading to arrange items in order according to the type of heading it is, such as Name or Artist.
Library	Stores and helps organize all the tracks on your computer.
Genius	Creates playlists using songs you have in your library that sound similar or go well together.

Table 6-1: *iTunes interface functions*

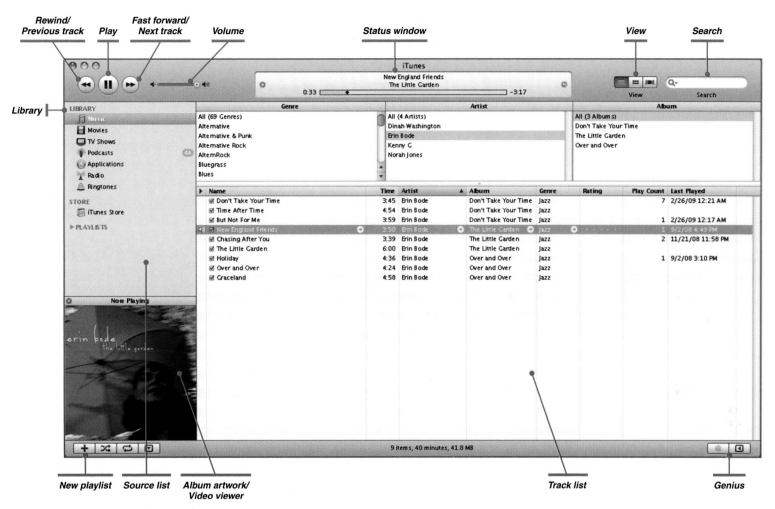

Rewind/
Previous track Play Fast forward/
Next track Volume Status window View Search

Library

LIBRARY
♫ Music
📺 Movies
📺 TV Shows
🎙 Podcasts
🎮 Applications
📻 Radio
🔔 Ringtones

STORE
🎵 iTunes Store

▶ PLAYLISTS

Now Playing

New playlist Source list Album artwork/
Video viewer Track list Genius

Figure 6-1: **The iTunes interface is simple to navigate, yet powerful to use.**

Import Audio into iTunes

Getting music into iTunes is simple, but there are various ways to do so. One way is to purchase music from the iTunes Store, but we'll cover that in the next section of this chapter. Right now, let's take a look at importing music from CDs and files.

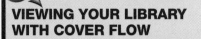

UICKSTEPS

VIEWING YOUR LIBRARY WITH COVER FLOW

Cover Flow is a cool way to view the items in your library by skimming through the album art. You can fly through the art by dragging the slider at the bottom of the window.

1. Open iTunes.

2. Click an item under Library in the source list (Music, Movies, etc.).

3. Select the **Cover Flow** icon on the right side of the View button, and your audio files will appear using Cover Flow.

IMPORTING FROM CDs

CDs appear to be going the way of the dinosaur, but you can preserve your music by importing it into iTunes.

1. Insert the CD into your computer's CD or DVD drive. The CD will show in the source list.

2. When the list of songs appears, clear the check box next to any songs you don't want to import.

3. To import the selected songs to your library, click the **Import CD** button in the lower-right corner of the window. You can cancel the import process by clicking the **X** next to the progress bar in the status window.

4. When the import is finished, click the **Eject** symbol to the right of the CD in the source list to remove the CD.

IMPORTING FROM FILES

Sometimes you may have audio files, such as MP3s or WAVs, that you want to import into iTunes. Doing so is just as simple as importing from a CD.

1. Click the **File** menu and select **Add To Library** (Mac) or **Add File To Library** (PC).

2. Browse your computer's hard drive for the audio file you want to import.

3. Select the file to import and click the **Open** button.

4. The audio will be added to your Music library.

TIP

You can also drag-and-drop songs from Finder (Mac) or Windows Explorer (Windows) into the iTunes window to add them to your library.

QUICKSTEPS

ADDING LYRICS TO YOUR SONGS

Do you ever try to sing along with your favorite songs, only to discover you might not remember the lyrics correctly? I've been guilty of belting out gibberish on more than one occasion when confronted with this issue. iTunes to the rescue! You can add lyrics to your favorite songs within iTunes.

1. Find the lyrics to the song in question on the Internet or in the CD's insert.

2. Click the song in your iTunes library to highlight it.

3. Choose the **File** menu and select **Get Info**.

4. Click the **Lyrics** tab.

5. Enter the lyrics into the text field, and then click **OK**.

Check Out the iTunes Store

The iTunes Store is your one-stop shop for all things digital media. Apple has provided a great place to find most (if not all) of your favorite music, movies, television shows, audiobooks, podcasts, and more. You can download single songs or entire albums, rent or buy movies, and subscribe to podcasts.

Subscribe to Podcasts

Podcasts are radio or video shows that you can download in iTunes and sync to your iPhone or iPod touch. This way, you can listen to or view your favorite

CONTINUING YOUR EDUCATION WITH iTUNES U

One of my favorite places to visit in the iTunes Store is iTunes U. Click the **iTunes U** link, and you will jump into a world of education opportunities offered from some of the world's most prestigious institutions of higher learning. Scroll down to the **Learn More** category and click **An Introduction To iTunes U** to learn more about this great (and free) section of the iTunes Store.

podcasts when it's convenient for you. Most popular radio shows can be found in the iTunes Store, and you can find podcasts for almost any subject you can think of.

1. Click the **iTunes Store** icon in the source list.

2. Select **Podcasts** from the iTunes Store categories on the left side of the iTunes window.

*Figure 6-2: **There is a literal plethora of podcasts to choose from in the iTunes Store Podcast Directory.***

3. Browse the hundreds of available podcasts (Figure 6-2) and click one you want to subscribe to.

TIP

Modify how often iTunes checks for new podcast episodes, as well as what it does with them when they are discovered, by selecting **Podcasts** in the source list and then clicking the **Settings** button.

4. Click the **Subscribe** button on the main page for the podcast. The most recent installment of the podcast will be downloaded to your computer. iTunes will automatically download new episodes of the podcast when they are available.

5. Click **Podcasts** in the source list to see which podcasts you are subscribed to and view the episodes you've downloaded for each one.

Sync Music with iTunes

Getting music into iTunes is just half the battle when you consider that this book is about iPhone and iPod touch. We need to get those groovy tunes synchronized with your device so you can listen on the go.

1. Connect your iPhone or iPod touch to your computer.
2. Click the device's icon in iTunes' source list.
3. Select the **Music** tab and determine how you want to sync your music.
4. Click the **Apply** button in the lower-right corner to begin the sync.

Create Playlists

Playlists are great for grouping individual songs into a collection. For instance, you could have a playlist dedicated to your favorite jazz songs, or another just for Elvis tunes.

1. Click the + button in the lower-left corner of the iTunes window.
2. Enter a name for your new playlist, which is shown in the Playlists section of the source list.
3. Click the Music library, select a song you want to add to the playlist, and drag-and-drop it onto the playlist's name. Hold down the COMMAND key (Mac) or CTRL key (Windows) while clicking to select multiple songs.

TURNING ON GENIUS PLAYLISTS

Genius creates playlists using songs that are already in your library that are similar to or sound good together. You must be connected to the Internet to use Genius.

1. Click the **Show Or Hide The Genius Sidebar** button in the lower-right corner of the iTunes window to open the Genius sidebar.

2. Click the **Turn On Genius** button to enable the feature in iTunes.

3. Choose a song from your Music library and click to highlight it.

4. Click the **Genius** button in the lower-right corner of the iTunes window to create the playlist.

Create Smart Playlists

Smart Playlists automatically search your library for songs that match the criteria you set when you created it. When you create a Smart Playlist, you set the rules that it must abide by when choosing songs to populate itself.

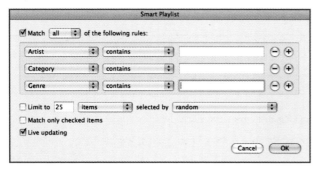

Figure 6-3: **Add or remove rules as necessary to customize your Smart Playlist.**

1. Click the **File** menu and select **New Smart Playlist**.

2. Determine whether songs should match all or any of the rules of your Smart Playlist.

3. Click the **+** or **−** buttons to add or remove rules (Figure 6-3).

4. iTunes automatically populates the Smart Playlist based on the rules you set for it.

TIP

You can edit your Smart Playlist's rules at any time by highlighting it in the source list, clicking the **File** menu, and choosing **Edit Smart Playlist**.

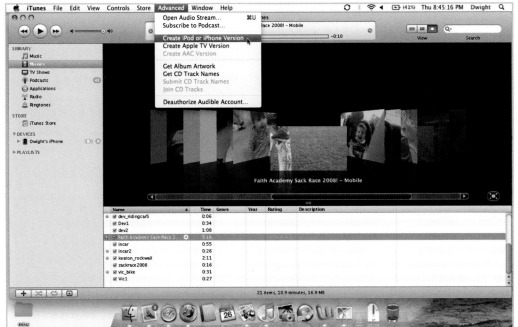

Format Movies for the iPhone/iPod touch with iTunes

A great feature I love in iTunes is the ability to format movies in your Movies library for optimum playback on your iPhone or iPod touch.

1. Select the **Movies** library in the source list.

2. Highlight the movie you want to format for your device.

3. Select the **Advanced** menu and choose **Create iPod Or iPhone Version**.

4. A newly formatted version of the movie will appear in the Movies library, ready to sync with your device.

QUICKSTEPS

COPYING PLAYLISTS TO YOUR DEVICE

You can copy easily an entire playlist from your computer to your iPhone or iPod touch.

1. Connect your device to the computer.

2. Find the playlist you want to copy to the device.

3. Drag-and-drop the playlist onto the device's name in the source list to copy the songs to the device. If any of the songs in the playlist already reside on the device, they won't be copied again, but the playlist and any other songs will still sync.

Rent or Buy Movies from the iTunes Store

The iTunes Store is not only your online music store; it's also the most convenient place to rent and buy movies that you can watch on your computer, television, iPhone, or iPod touch. You'll find lots to choose from, whether time-tested classics, recent Oscar winners, or the newest releases. Every category is available, too, from the geekiest of science fiction to the most endearing family entertainment.

1. Select **iTunes Store** in the source list.

2. Click the **Movies** link under the iTunes Store category.

3. Browse the huge selection for movies that strike your fancy. Click a movie's title to open its main page in the iTunes Store.

4. Click the **View Trailer** button to see the theatrical trailer for the film, or click the **Rent** or **Buy** button.

Sync Video with iTunes

Getting video from iTunes is just as simple as syncing music. Having a good movie to watch can really help pass the time on a long road trip or plane flight, especially where children are involved.

1. Connect your iPhone or iPod touch to your computer.

2. Click the device's icon in iTunes' source list.

3. Select the **Video** tab (iPhone) or **Movies** tab (iPod touch) and determine which movies to sync with your device.

4. Click the **Apply** button in the lower-right corner to begin the sync.

Enjoy Media on Your iPhone 3G/iPod touch

Now that you've gotten the basics of getting media to your device, it's time to find out how to enjoy it. It's amazing how we can fit all that entertainment (and hopefully some education, too) into such a tiny device and carry it with us wherever we go!

- To access audio and video on your iPhone, just touch the **iPod** icon in the Dock.
- To see your audio files on an iPod touch, tap the **Music** icon in the Dock; to view movies, tap the **Video** icon.

Browse Playlists, Artists, and Songs

When you tap the iPod or Music button (depending on the device you have), you will see a screen much like that in Figure 6-4. Things look similar between the iPhone and iPod touch, with the one exception that there is no Video button on the iPod touch.

Figure 6-4: ***Touch an option at the bottom of the screen to browse your audio files.***

PLAYLISTS

Touch the Playlists button at the bottom of the screen to see playlists you created in iTunes and synced with your device.

1. Flick your finger up and down to browse the playlists.

2. Tap a playlist to see its contents.

3. Touch the name of a song to begin playing it.

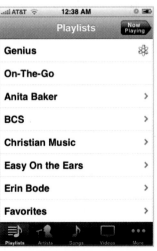

TIP

You can browse the rest of your library, even if a song is currently playing. To immediately jump back to the song that's playing, touch the **Now Playing** button in the upper-right corner of the screen.

ARTISTS

Touch the Artists button at the bottom of the screen to sort music according to the name of the artist.

1. Tap the artist's name to see albums associated with it.

2. Touch an album name to see the music contained therein.

3. Tap the song name to begin playing it.

SONGS

The Songs button will display all the songs in your library in alphabetical order. Simply touch a song to play it.

Organize Albums, Audiobooks, Compilations, Composers, Genres, and Podcasts

Tap the More button in the lower-right corner of the screen to see more options for viewing the items in your library (Figure 6-5).

- Tap the **Albums** button to see all the album collections in your library.

- Touch **Audiobooks** to listen to any audiobooks you may have purchased from the iTunes Store.

- Touch **Compilations**, **Composers**, or **Genres** to see audio that is part of a compilation, arranged by a particular composer, or that belongs to a certain genre of music.

- Listen to podcasts you subscribe to by tapping the **Podcasts** button, selecting a podcast, and then choosing an episode from the podcast.

*Figure 6-5: **There are several options for sorting the audio content of your device.***

UICKSTEPS

DOWNLOADING PODCASTS WITH YOUR iPHONE 3G/iPOD TOUCH

You can download podcasts in iTunes and sync them with your device, or you can download podcasts directly to your iPhone or iPod touch via your wireless network.

1. Tap the **iTunes** icon on the Home screen.

2. Touch the **Podcasts** icon on the toolbar at the bottom of the screen.

3. Browse the Podcast Directory using the **What's Hot**, **Top Tens**, and **Categories** tabs at the top of the screen.

4. Once you've found a podcast that suits your fancy, tap its name to see its main page.

5. Find an episode you'd like to download and tap the **Free** button next to it.

6. Tap the **Download** button to begin downloading the episode.

7. The Downloads icon in the lower-right corner indicates you have a download taking place. Once the download is finished, you can access the podcasts using the iPod or Music app on your device.

Understand the Playback Controls

iPhone and iPod touch offer several controls to give you command when playing songs on your device. Figure 6-6 points out the major items of interest in the playback window.

Figure 6-6: **The playback controls help you control the action.**

TIP

Tap the album art in the playback window to see additional controls, such as a scrubber to jump to a particular place in the song, repeat the music, shuffle the songs, or create a Genius playlist based on the song currently playing.

Browse Your Music with Cover Flow

You've seen how easy and functional, not to mention just plain cool, it is to browse your music in iTunes using Cover Flow, right? Well, guess what? You can do the same with your iPhone or iPod touch, too!

1. Touch the **iPod** icon (iPhone) or the **Music** icon (iPod touch).
2. Turn your device sideways, and your music will be displayed by its album art.

3. Browse the collection by dragging or flicking your fingers to the left or right.
4. Tap an album to see the songs contained in it.
5. Touch a song to play it.

CONFIGURING THE TOOLBAR

Don't like the choices you have in the main toolbar? You can change your view quite easily, thank you very much.

1. Touch the **iPod** icon (iPhone) or the **Music** icon (iPod touch).
2. Tap the **More** button.
3. Press the **Edit** button in the upper-left corner.
4. In the Configure window, drag an item you want to use and drop it on top of the icon you want it to replace in the toolbar (bottom of the screen).

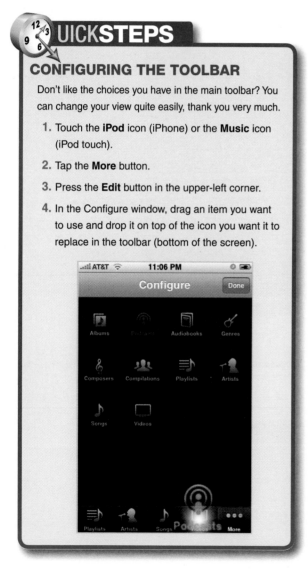

Watch Video on Your iPhone 3G/iPod touch

Watching video on your device is similar to listening to music. To see the videos on your device:

- For iPhone, touch the **iPod** button in the Dock and then tap the **Video** icon in the toolbar.
- For iPod touch, touch the **Video** button in the Dock.

Scroll through the list of available videos and tap the one you would like to view. Rotate your device sideways to view the video, and use the controls in the playback window to customize the experience. It's just that simple!

How to...

* *Take Pictures with the Camera*
* *Record Video with the Camera*
* *View Your Pictures and Videos*
* *Sync Your Photos with a Computer Using iTunes*
* *Import Photos and Videos to a Mac Using iPhoto*
* *Manually Import Photos and Videos to a Computer*
* *Add Photo Albums with iPhoto*
* *Add Photos and Videos to a MobileMe Gallery*
* *Sharing an Album on MobileMe*
* *View a Slideshow*
* *Setting Slideshow Preferences*
* *Playing Music with Your Slideshow*
* *E-mail a Photo or Video*
* *Send a Photo or Video via SMS or MMS*
* *Adding a Picture Within a Contact Record*
* *Assign a Photo to a Contact*
* *Set a Picture as Wallpaper*
* *Taking Screen Shots*
* *Delete Unwanted Pictures and Videos*

Chapter 7

Taking and Managing Photos

Your iPhone is capable of snapping some pretty nifty pictures and capturing video (iPhone 3GS only) of whatever or whomever you see fit to point it at. After a few clicks of the camera, you'll want to share your pics with all of your friends, and there are multiple ways to do so: e-mail, MobileMe, and even text messaging (sort of). You can also assign pictures to contacts, create slideshows, and copy pictures to your computer for editing and printing.

While you can't take pictures with your iPod touch, you can put pictures on the device and carry them with you. The Photos app works the same on the iPod touch as it does on the iPhone, with the exception that pictures stored in the iPod touch have been imported from your computer, whereas the iPhone can contain pictures from your computer and camera.

Become an iPhone Paparazzi

The built-in camera on your iPhone takes surprisingly good pictures, and I don't say that as a slight, but to compliment Apple. Considering that there is no zoom or flash and that the only resolutions available are 2.0 megapixels for the iPhone 3G and 3.0 megapixels for the iPhone 3GS, the results you'll achieve will be a good bit better than you might expect.

Take Pictures with the Camera

Taking pictures with your iPhone may take a little getting used to at first. There is no physical button to push to take the shots; you must touch a button on the touchscreen to take the pictures.

1. From the Home screen, touch the **Camera** button to launch the app.

2. When the app first opens, you will see a closed camera shutter.

3. The shutter will open and display what your cameras lens is seeing.

4. Point the camera at your subject, and tap the **Camera** button at the bottom of the screen (Figure 7-1).

5. iPhone 3GS owners, make sure the switch in the lower right of the screen is set to Photo, not Video (tap it to change between the two settings).

6. The shutter will close as the picture is taken and then quickly reopen. Your picture has been saved in the Camera Roll.

Record Video with the Camera

The iPhone 3GS owners in the audience have the added bonus of being able to record video with their device. Again, there is no physical button to push to record the video, so it might take some getting used to before you are comfortable recording video with your iPhone 3GS.

TIP

Turn the camera sideways to take landscape shots. You'll notice the camera icon on the Camera button will flip on its side as well.

Figure 7-1: ***Tap the Camera button, and you will hear the sound of a shutter!***

1. From the Home screen, touch the **Camera** button to launch the app.

2. When the shutter opens, be certain the Photo/Video switch is set to video (if not, simply tap it).

3. Tap the Record button to begin recording your video.

4. When finished recording, tap the Record button again.

View Your Pictures and Videos

Once you've taken a few good snapshots and recordings, it's always a good idea to check out your handiwork. You can view pictures and videos stored on your iPhone in one of two ways: from within the Camera app or using the Photos app. iPod touch users can use the Photos app to see pictures they've imported to their device.

VIEW PICS WITH THE CAMERA APP

To view your pictures while using the Camera app:

1. Tap the **thumbnail image** in the lower-left corner of the screen (Figure 7-2).

Figure 7-2: **Tap this icon to view your Camera Roll.**

2. The Camera Roll window opens, revealing all the pictures and videos it contains.

3. Scroll through your pictures and videos by flicking your finger up or down on the screen.

4. Tap a picture or video to view it full screen.

5. Turn the iPhone sideways to better view landscape images and videos.

6. Tap pictures and videos once to hide the controls, and tap again to bring them back up.

7. Tap the **Done** button in the upper-right corner of the screen to return to Camera mode.

VIEWING PICS WITH THE PHOTOS APP

To view your pictures utilizing the Photos app:

1. From the Home screen, tap the **Photos** button to open the Photo Albums screen.

2. On the Photo Albums screen, touch an album to view its contents.

3. Scroll through the pictures and videos in the album by flicking your finger up or down on the touchscreen.

4. Tap a picture or video to view it full screen. Turn your device sideways to get a better look at landscape images and recordings.

5. Tap the picture or video once to hide the controls, and then tap again to show them.

6. Touch the button in the upper-left corner of the screen to return to the previous album or to return to the Photo Albums window. The name of the button you see is determined by whether you're viewing an individual picture or an album's contents.

Move Your Pictures and Videos to a Computer

The iPhone's built-in camera affords you the convenience of being able to take a picture or record a video whenever the fancy strikes; no need to carry a camera with you at all times. Sometimes, though, just having the pictures and/or recordings on your iPhone isn't as good as having them on your computer. Once the pics and videos are on your computer, you can edit them and print them out (pictures, not videos), which are two tasks you can't accomplish on the iPhone (at least not without third-party software). In this section of the chapter, we'll see how to utilize several methods to successfully copy your stills and recordings to your computer, whether you use a Mac or a Windows-based PC, as well as getting pictures from your computer to your device.

Sync Your Photos with a Computer Using iTunes

You knew our trusty friend, iTunes, would be involved in this somehow, didn't you? iTunes is the main conduit for your computer to talk to your iPhone or iPod touch. It offers a way for you to synchronize pictures stored in a folder or within a photo application on your computer with the device of your choice. Supported applications include:

- iPhoto 4.03 or later (Mac)
- Aperture (Mac)
- Adobe Photoshop Album 2.0 or later (PC)
- Adobe Photoshop Elements 3.0 or later (PC)

To sync using iTunes:

1. Connect your device to the computer and launch iTunes (if it doesn't open automatically).

2. Select your device in the source list.

3. Click the **Photos** tab to see the available options.

4. Select the **Sync Photos From** check box.

5. Select either an application or a folder from the Sync Photos From pop-up menu.

6. Decide whether to sync all photos, all or some events, or only selected folders, and click the appropriate radio button and check boxes, if needed.

7. Click **Apply** in the lower-right corner.

8. Click **Sync** in the lower-right corner to begin the synchronization process.

NOTE

Videos cannot be synced with the iPhone 3GS.

NOTE

Folders will be copied to your device and listed as photo albums in the Photos app, as are albums synchronized from applications.

Import Photos and Videos to a Mac Using iPhoto

If you are a lucky Mac user who owns a copy of the iLife suite of applications, you have in your possession a copy of iPhoto, which is Apple's great photo management application. iPhoto knows how to play nice with your iPhone and will allow you to download pictures and videos from it into your Mac's Photo library with incredible ease.

1. Connect your iPhone to your Mac.

2. Launch iPhoto by double-clicking its icon in the Applications folder, or single-clicking it if an iPhoto icon resides in the Dock.

3. A few seconds after iPhoto launches, you will see your iPhone in the source list on the left side of the window, much like you do in iTunes. Click the iPhone to see pictures and videos you haven't synchronized.

4. To import all the pictures and videos, simply click the **Import All** button.

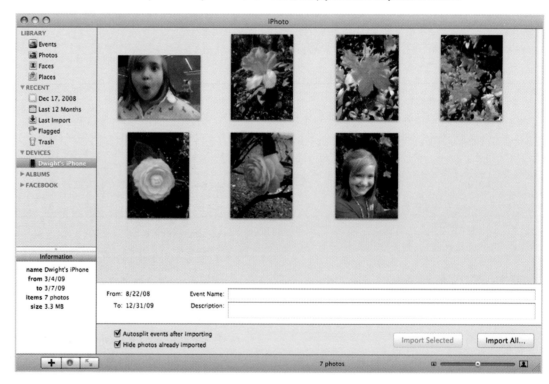

5. To import individual pictures or videos, hold down the **COMMAND (or APPLE)** key on your keyboard while clicking the pictures and videos you want. Once selection is complete, click the **Import Selected** button.

6. When the import is finished, you will be asked whether you want to delete the pictures or videos from your iPhone or leave them on it. Make a choice and click the appropriate button. If you want to copy the pictures and videos to another device, it's best that you leave them on the iPhone, but if you don't need to do so, you can free up that much more memory on your iPhone by deleting them.

7. The newly imported pictures and videos can be seen in the Events and Photos libraries, as well as by clicking **Last Import** in the source list.

Manually Import Photos and Videos to a Computer

When I say "manually import," I mean to copy pictures to and from your device, and even delete pictures from the device, with nothing more than the tools that came with your computer's operating system (no need for third-party or additional applications). Let's see how to perform this minor miracle with Mac OS X and Windows Vista.

IMPORT WITH WINDOWS VISTA

1. Connect your device to your computer.

2. Click **Start** and choose **Computer**.

3. Double-click the **Apple iPhone** icon (it looks like a camera) under Portable Devices.

4. Double-click **Internal Storage**.

5. Double-click the **DCIM** folder.

6. Double-click the **100APPLE** folder to view the pictures on your device.

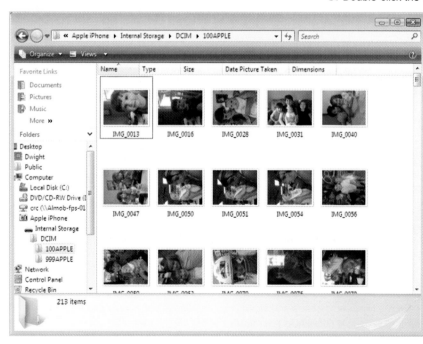

7. Drag-and-drop pics and videos to import them one at a time, or press **CTRL+A** to select all and drag them to a folder.

8. To automatically import to a particular folder on the computer, right-click the **Apple iPhone** icon under Portable Devices, select **Import Pictures** from the menu, and then click **Import** in the Importing Pictures And Videos window.

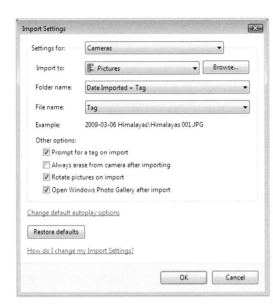

9. Click the **Options** link in the lower-left corner of the Importing Pictures And Videos window to change the settings for your import, such as the default import folder.

IMPORT WITH MAC OS X

1. Connect your device to your Mac.

2. Open the Image Capture application by double-clicking its icon in the Applications folder.

3. Image Capture should automatically recognize your device and open a window for it (Figure 7-3). If not, disconnect and reconnect your device.

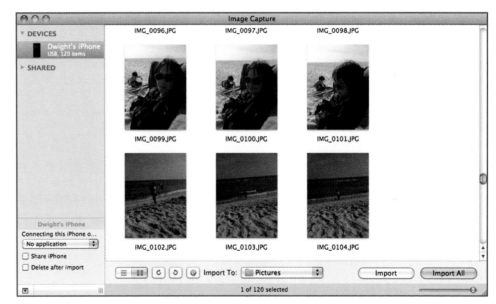

Figure 7-3: **You can perform several tasks, such as downloading your pictures, using this window.**

4. Select a download location for your pictures and videos using the **Import To** pop-up menu at the bottom of the window.

5. To import all of your pictures at one time, click the **Import All** button.

TIP

If you are connecting your iPhone or iPod touch through a USB hub and it's not being recognized by Image Capture, try connecting directly to the USB ports on your Mac or PC.

6. Download individual pictures by holding down the **COMMAND** key while clicking the individual pictures, and click the **Import** button when ready to begin the import.

Add Photo Albums with iPhoto

You may want to organize your pictures into albums so that you can browse them easily on your iPhone or iPod touch. You can easily create photo albums with iPhoto and sync the albums using iTunes.

1. Open iPhoto.

2. Click the **+** button in the lower-left corner of the window.

3. Select **Album** from the toolbar and give the new album a name.

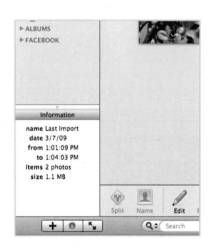

4. Click Create to make the new album appear under the Albums item in the source list.

5. Drag pictures from other items in the source list to the new album.

6. Open iTunes and select the **Photos** tab.

7. Choose **iPhoto** in the Sync Photos From pop-up menu. The new album will appear in the window.

8. Click **Apply** if you've made changes, and then click **Sync**. The new album will now be in your device's Photos app for your viewing pleasure.

Add Photos and Videos to a MobileMe Gallery

MobileMe is a paid service from Apple that has revolutionized the way we keep our information synchronized across multiple devices, such as computers and cell phones. One cool feature of MobileMe is that you can upload pictures and/or videos on your iPhone or iPod touch with a gallery on your MobileMe account. This way, you can easily share your photos and videos via the Internet.

1. Open a web browser on your Mac or PC and go to www.me.com.

NOTE

If you don't already have a MobileMe account, you can try the service for free by visiting www.apple.com/mobileme and clicking the **Free Trial** button.

2. Enter your member name and password into the appropriate fields, and then click the **Log In** button.

3. Click the **Photos** icon in the upper-left corner of the window to open the MobileMe Gallery page.

4. Click the **+** button in the lower-left corner to create a new album.

5. In the Album Settings window (Figure 7-4), give your new album a name, select the **Adding Of Photos Via E-mail Or iPhone** check box, and then click **Create**.

6. On your iPhone or iPod touch, open the Photos app and select the album that contains the picture or video you want to upload to MobileMe.

7. Tap the picture or video you want to upload to view it in full screen.

8. Tap the **Action** button in the lower-left corner of the screen.

9. Tap the Send To MobileMe button.

10. Select an album in your MobileMe Gallery in which to place the picture/video, and enter a title and description.

Album Settings

Album Name: Vic in Spring

Allow: ☐ Downloading of photos or entire album
☐ Uploading of photos via web browser
☑ Adding of photos via email or iPhone
Address will be available after publishing

Show: ☐ Photo titles
☐ Email address for uploading photos

Advanced: ☐ Hide album on my Gallery page

Cancel   Create

Figure 7-4: Configure the settings for your new album, being certain to allow for uploading from an iPhone.

11. Tap the **Publish** button to upload the picture. iPhone will tell you when the item has been published to the selected gallery.

12. Go back to your MobileMe Gallery in your web browser. Click the album you uploaded the picture to, and the picture or video should show up there.

Work with Pictures and Videos on Your Device

There are lots of things you can do with your pictures and videos on your iPhone or iPod touch. You can view slideshows of your albums, e-mail pictures and videos to friends, send photos using text messaging, assign a picture to a contact, and set pictures to be wallpaper on your device.

SHARING AN ALBUM ON MOBILEME

You can easily share your MobileMe albums with friends and family, and they can subscribe to the album so that they can keep up with your newest additions.

1. From within your favorite web browser, log in to your MobileMe account and open Gallery.

2. Click the name of the album to display its contents.

3. Copy the URL in the upper-right corner of the Gallery window, and e-mail it to someone you want to share the album with.

4. The recipients of your e-mail can simply click the link you sent to them, and they can now view your album online.

5. Depending on the settings you gave your album, viewers of the album can browse its contents, subscribe to the album, download pictures from it, and even upload pictures into it.

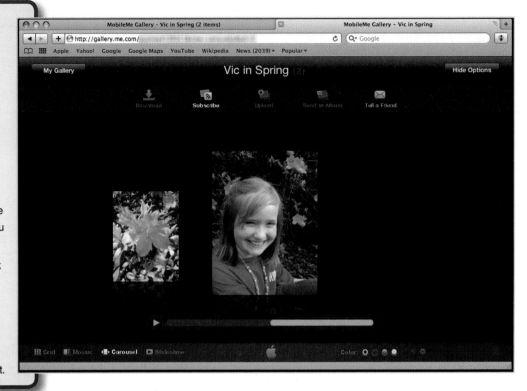

View a Slideshow

Impress your friends and family by showing your pictures with a slideshow, complete with cool transition effects.

1. Open the Photos app.

2. Select an album containing photos you want to view.

3. Tap the first photo you want to view in the slideshow.

4. Tap the **Play** button at the bottom of the screen to begin the slideshow. You can scroll through the slideshow by flicking the screen to the right or left.

5. Stop the slideshow at any time by simply tapping the screen.

You can customize how a slideshow plays by adjusting the preferences.

1. From the Home screen, tap the **Settings** icon.

2. Scroll down the screen and touch the **Photos** button.

3. Modify any settings you wish, such as the duration a slide should play and the type of transition effect to use (Ripple is really neat).

4. Tap the **Home** button when finished making changes.

...ıll AT&T 🔛	12:36 PM	◯ 🔋
Settings	**Photos**	
Slideshow		
Play Each Slide For	3 Seconds	›
Transition	Ripple	›
Repeat	OFF	
Shuffle	OFF	

QUICK**FACTS**

PLAYING MUSIC WITH YOUR SLIDESHOW

You can add a little ambience to your slideshow by playing a favorite tune along with it. Open the iPod app (iPhone) or Music app (iPod touch), begin playing a song, and then go to Photos and begin your slideshow.

E-mail a Photo or Video

Send your favorite folks the latest and greatest picture or video you've taken via e-mail. This is a good method for sending them a photo or video that they can download and keep on their computer.

1. Open the Photos app and select an album.

2. Tap the picture or video you want to e-mail.

3. Touch the **Action** button in the lower-left corner of the screen.

4. Select **E-mail Photo/Video**.

5. When the Mail app opens a new e-mail containing your picture, enter the addresses of your intended recipients.

6. Add a subject and a message, if you like.

7. Click **Send** when you're ready to deliver the e-mail.

Send a Photo or Video via SMS or MMS

The Messages app on your iPhone is capable of sending text messages via Short Messaging Service (SMS), and supports the sending of multimedia messages with Multimedia Messaging Service (MMS). Unfortunately as of this writing, MMS is not supported by the wireless carrier in the United States, so I will show our American readers a tricky little way to work around this contrived limitation (using e-mail), as well as show those of you lucky enough to have MMS capabilities the intended way to perform the task.

SENDING MULTIMEDIA WITH MMS IN THE UNITED STATES

1. Open the picture you'd like to send via MMS.

2. Tap the **Action** button in the lower-left corner of the screen and touch the **E-mail Photo** button.

CARRIER	MMS ADDRESS FORMAT
Alltel	number@message.alltel.com
AT&T	number@mms.att.net
Boost Mobile	number@myboostmobile.com
Sprint	number@messaging.sprintpcs.com
T-Mobile	number@tmomail.net
Verizon	number@vzwpix.com

Table 7-1: Cellular Carrier MMS Address Formats

QUICKSTEPS

ADDING A PICTURE WITHIN A CONTACT RECORD

You can easily add a picture to a contact from within the contact record itself.

1. Open a contact record from within an app.

2. Tap the **Edit** button in the upper-right corner.

3. Touch the **Add Photo** box in the upper-left corner of the screen.

4. Tap the **Take Photo** button to use the camera to take a snapshot of your subject, or tap the **Choose Existing Photo** button to use a picture already stored on your device.

3. Enter the MMS address of the intended recipient in the To field using Table 7-1 as a guide. Type the complete phone number (no dashes), including the area code, followed by the MMS address format. The format will vary, depending on the recipient's cellular carrier.

4. Tap the **Send** button to deliver the message.

SENDING MULTIMEDIA WITH MMS OUTSIDE THE UNITED STATES

1. Open the picture you'd like to send via MMS.

2. Tap the **Action** button in the lower-left corner of the screen and touch the **MMS** button.

3. Select a recipient for your message and tap **Send**.

Assign a Photo to a Contact

Assigning a picture to a contact helps you instantly recognize whom you're receiving a call from, and it's quite simple to set up.

1. Open the picture you want to use for the contact.

2. Tap the picture and touch the **Action** button in the lower-left corner.

3. Tap the **Assign To Contact** button.

4. Scroll through the list of contacts and tap the one you want to assign the picture to.

5. In the Move And Scale screen, drag the picture to position it the way you like. You can also zoom in on a particular area of the picture.

6. Tap the **Set Photo** button to complete the process.

Set a Picture as Wallpaper

You can decorate your computer's desktop with wallpaper, and you can do the same for your iPhone or iPod touch.

1. Open the picture you want to use as wallpaper.

2. Tap the picture and touch the **Action** button in the lower-left corner.

TAKING SCREEN SHOTS

Just as you can take screen shots of items on your computer's display, you can also take shots of your iPhone or iPod touch's screen. Simply press the **Sleep/Wake** button and the **Home** button simultaneously. Your screen will flash white, and the screen shot will be added to your Camera Roll.

3. Tap the **Use As Wallpaper** button.

4. In the Move And Scale screen, position the picture or zoom in on a particular part of it.

5. Tap the **Set Wallpaper** button in the lower-right corner to use the picture as your wallpaper.

Delete Unwanted Pictures and Videos

Last, but not least, we learn how to get rid of pictures and video recordings we no longer want on our iPhone or iPod touch. There's nothing to it.

1. Open the Photos app.

2. Tap the album containing the picture or video we want to take a hike.

3. Tap the offending picture/video to view it full screen.

4. Tap the **Trashcan** icon in the lower-right corner of the screen.

5. Touch the **Delete Photo/Video** button to send the picture packing.

There is no way to recover a deleted photo or video! You will have to sync with your Mac or PC again to get pictures/videos back on your device. If you've never synced the photo or uploaded the video to your computer, it will be gone forever.

How to...

- **Get Today's Forecast with Weather**
- **Viewing Temps in Fahrenheit or Celsius**
- **Getting More Information About a Location**
- **Organize Your Thoughts with Notes**
- **Manage Your Time with Clock**
- **Communicate with Messages**
- **Get Where You're Going with Maps**
- **Viewing Satellite Images**
- **Using Location Services with Your Device**
- **Finding Your Current Location**
- **Finding a Local Business**
- **Add It All Up with Calculator**
- **Watch Videos with YouTube**
- **Keep Up (and Down) with Your Stocks**
- **Track Appointments with Calendar**
- **Manage Contacts**
- **Searching for Items on Your Device**
- **Create Reminders with Voice Memos**

Chapter 8

Using Applications that Make Your Life Easier

The apps that come with your iPhone or iPod touch are really great at helping you with daily tasks, keeping up with your stock portfolio, and organizing your thoughts. You can also get driving directions and maps, keep tabs on the weather, and watch the latest uploads to YouTube. Practicality, usefulness, and a little entertainment sums up the description of apps you get with your device right out of the box. This chapter aims to give you an overview of these apps and make you more familiar with their capabilities.

Apps for Everyday Life

Applications such as Weather, Notes, Clock, Text, Maps, Calculator, and YouTube will quickly become your good buddies once you learn more about them. In this section we'll see what these apps can do for you, as well as learn how to configure them to work the way you need.

Get Today's Forecast with Weather

It's always nice to know what to expect when it comes to the weather, especially when you're on the road or have a special outdoor event planned. The Weather app that comes with your iPhone or iPod touch gives you instant access to the latest forecasts.

CHECK THE WEATHER

1. Open Weather by tapping its icon on the Home screen.

2. Weather displays the current temperature and conditions, as well as forecasts for the next six days, as seen in Figure 8-1. My iPhone had Cupertino, California (the home of Apple's headquarters), set as its default weather location.

ADD NEW LOCATIONS

You may want to keep up with the weather in more than one location, and the Weather app makes it easy to add cities to your list of locations.

1. Open Weather.

2. Tap the **information** icon (*i*) in the lower-right corner of the screen.

3. Tap the **+** button in the upper-left corner of the Weather screen.

Today's high and low temps | Current conditions | Current temperature

Forecast

Figure 8-1: **Layout of the Weather app's main screen**

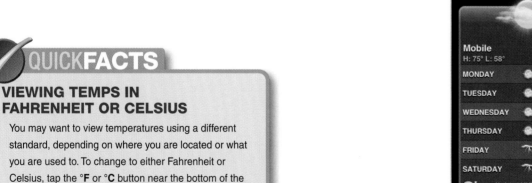

4. Enter the name of a city and state, or enter the city's zip code, and tap the **Search** button in the lower-right corner. Weather will search for locations as you type; simply tap the item you want if it appears in the list before you finish entering the name.

5. The new city is now added to your list of locations.

6. Arrange the cities in order of importance by touching the three bars to the right of one of the cities and dragging the city up or down to a new location in the list.

7. Tap the **Done** button in the upper-right corner to finish adding locations.

NAVIGATE MULTIPLE LOCATIONS

You can see the weather information for only one location at a time, but you can easily see the other locations you keep up with.

1. Open Weather.

2. Note the small dots at the bottom of the screen. Those dots represent the cities in your location list.

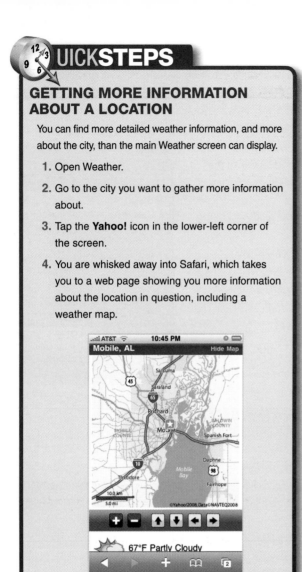

QUICKSTEPS

GETTING MORE INFORMATION ABOUT A LOCATION

You can find more detailed weather information, and more about the city, than the main Weather screen can display.

1. Open Weather.

2. Go to the city you want to gather more information about.

3. Tap the **Yahoo!** icon in the lower-left corner of the screen.

4. You are whisked away into Safari, which takes you to a web page showing you more information about the location in question, including a weather map.

3. Tap the dots to move from one city to the next.

4. Scroll through your cities by flicking your finger to the right or left on the screen.

DELETING A CITY

Deleting a city from your locations list is as simple as can be.

1. Open Weather.

2. Tap the **information** button (*i*) in the lower-right corner.

3. Tap the **red circle** to the left of the city you want to remove from the list.

4. Tap the **Delete** button displayed to the right of the city's name.

Organize Your Thoughts with Notes

Ah, if I only had a dollar for every great idea that just floated away in the ether of my mind when I was unable to quickly jot it down! How nice it would be to remember something you've been wracking your brain over and be able to immediately make a notation of it so that it doesn't vanish into thin air.

x

Your iPhone or iPod touch has just the app to help you in these situations: the Notes app. Notes is as simple to use as a notepad, and you won't have to frantically search your pockets or purse for a pen.

1. Open Notes by tapping its icon on the Home screen.

2. If you don't have any notes, you will be prompted to create a new one. Use the keyboard to jot down whatever information or idea you have, and click the **Done** button in the upper-right corner when you are finished.

3. Tap the **Notes** button in the upper-left corner to view your notepad.

4. Tap a note in the notepad to view its contents.

5. Tap the **left** and **right** arrows at the bottom of the screen (when viewing a note) to move to the previous or next note.

When it comes to note creation and viewing notes, that's about all there is. But that's not all there is to the Notes app. Let's see what else we can do with Notes.

- E-mail a note to someone by simply tapping the **envelope** icon at the bottom of the screen while viewing a note. Enter the recipient's e-mail address, and tap the **Send** button in the upper-right corner.

- Delete unwanted notes by viewing them and tapping the **trashcan** icon; then tap the **Delete Note** button in the confirmation screen. The unfortunate note gets sucked into the trashcan and is gone for good.

- Add new notes by tapping the **+** button in the upper-right corner of the main notepad screen.

Manage Your Time with Clock

A clock may seem like a mundane item on a device as cool as an iPhone or iPod touch, but prepare to be surprised a bit. There are no earth-shattering functions introduced, mind you, but the Clock app does more than just tell time, as you're about to see. To get started, open Clock by tapping its icon on the Home screen.

WORLD CLOCK

The World Clock feature of the Clock app lets you view the time in other cities around this little blue globe we all spin around on.

1. Tap the **World Clock** icon in the lower-left corner of the screen.

2. Tap the **+** button in the upper-right corner to add a city.

3. Enter the name of a city using the onscreen keyboard, and tap the name once you see it in the list.

4. The new clock will appear in the World Clock screen. If the clock's face is white, it is daytime in the city; if it is black, it's nighttime.

5. Tap the **Edit** button in the upper-left corner of the World Clock screen to rearrange or remove cities in the list.

- Rearrange the order of cities in the list by dragging the **three bars** to the right of the city's name up or down in the list.

- Remove a city from the list by tapping the **red circle** to the left of its name and then tapping the **Delete** button to its right.

ALARM

The Alarm function of Clock is one of my favorite tools on my iPhone (no kidding). It's what wakes me up every morning and also reminds me of other tasks I need to perform during the day.

1. Tap the **Alarm** button at the bottom of Clock's screen.

2. Tap the **+** button in the upper-right corner to add an alarm to the list.

3. Modify the settings for your new alarm.
   - Touch the **Repeat** button to have the alarm repeated on certain days if you like.
   - Set an alarm sound by tapping the **Sound** button and choosing from the audio options.
   - Allow yourself an extra 10 minutes to wake up by turning on the **Snooze** option.
   - Assign a name to the alarm by tapping the **Label** button and entering the name with the keyboard.
   - Drag the time wheels at the bottom of the screen to set the time for your alarm.

4. Turn an alarm on or off by toggling its **On/Off** switch.

5. To make changes to an alarm, tap the **Edit** button in the upper-left corner and then tap the alarm's name.

6. To delete an alarm, tap the **Edit** button in the upper-left corner of the screen, tap the **red circle** to the left of the alarm's name, and then touch the **Delete** button to its right.

CAUTION

Don't forget to set whether the alarm is to go off in the A.M. or P.M.!

NOTE

An alarm icon appears next to the battery icon in the upper-right corner as a reminder that you have an alarm set.

STOPWATCH

You know, things don't get much simpler to operate than the Stopwatch in the Clock app, but it's a handy utility to have around should you have the sudden urge to time your 100-meter dash.

1. Open Stopwatch by tapping its icon in the bottom of the Clock screen.
2. To begin timing an event, tap the **Start** button.
3. If you are timing laps, tap the **Lap** button at the end of each lap to keep a record of time for each lap.
4. Touch the **Stop** button to stop the clock.
5. Select the **Reset** button to start the clock over at 00:00.0.

TIMER

Timer is another really simple, but ultimately useful, function of the Clock app, although it may not garner attention in the latest television ad for the iPhone or iPod touch.

1. Open Timer by tapping its icon in the lower-right corner of the screen.
2. Set the target time using the hours and minutes wheels; just flick your finger up or down on each to choose a time.
3. Tap the **When Timer Ends** button to choose an alarm sound that will go off when the timer has reached 0.
4. Touch the **Start** button to begin the countdown.
5. Tap the **Cancel** button if you want to end the countdown before it's finished.

Communicate with Messages

Exchanging text messages has become a communications phenomenon in the last few years. Some people actually prefer texting to placing a phone call.

It's an easy way to send out a quick message and get a quick response, without the pleasantries of an actual conversation.

1. Open Messages by tapping its icon on the Home screen.

2. In the Text Messages screen, tap the **new message** icon in the upper-right corner.

3. In the New Message screen, tap the **To** field and enter the recipient's name using the keyboard. If the recipient is in your contacts list, the name will appear as you type.

4. Add more than one recipient by tapping the **+** button in the right corner of the To field.

5. Touch the text field immediately above the keyboard, and begin entering the body of your message. When finished tap the **Send** button.

6. When your recipient responds, you will see each other's messages on the screen, with your text and theirs stored in balloons.

> **NOTE**
>
> As of this writing, those of us in the United States cannot send multimedia messages with the Messages program. Though it is a feature supported by Messages, MMS is not currently activated by our wireless carriers. See Chapter 7 for instructions on sending multimedia messages using Mail.

> **NOTE**
>
> The iPod touch must have access to the Internet via a wireless network in order to use Maps.

Get Where You're Going with Maps

Good news for all the guys who hate asking for directions: The Maps app is just what you've always needed! Maps allows you to view street maps and get directions, and even determine your current location. You can also view your map using satellite images!

VIEW A MAP OF A LOCATION

You can view detailed maps of a location, zoom in and out of those maps, and even use satellite imagery to see landmarks.

1. Open Maps by tapping its icon on the Home screen.

2. Touch the **search** field at the top of the screen to open the keyboard.

3. Type the address you want to find, or enter an intersection, contact name, zip code, bookmarked location, area, or landmark. Then tap the **Search** button.

4. When Maps finds the location, it marks it with a pin. Touch the pin to see the name of the location.

5. Tap the **blue circle containing the arrow** to see more information about the location, or tap the **orange android** icon to see a 360-degree street-level view of your location.

6. Zoom in on the map by pinching your fingers together and placing them on the screen and then spreading them apart (while still touching the screen). Zoom back out by spreading your fingers apart and placing them on the screen and then pinching your fingers together (again, while still touching the screen).

DROP PINS TO MARK A LOCATION

Maps lets you use pins to mark favorite locations.

1. Tap the **page** button in the lower-right corner of the screen.

2. Touch the **Drop Pin** button.

3. Drag the new pin to the location you prefer.

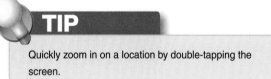

TIP
Quickly zoom in on a location by double-tapping the screen.

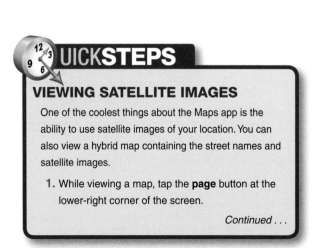

QUICKSTEPS

VIEWING SATELLITE IMAGES

One of the coolest things about the Maps app is the ability to use satellite images of your location. You can also view a hybrid map containing the street names and satellite images.

1. While viewing a map, tap the **page** button at the lower-right corner of the screen.

Continued ...

4. Move the pin by touching and dragging it to a new location.

UICK**STEPS**

VIEWING SATELLITE IMAGES

(Continued)

2. Touch the **Satellite** button to see a satellite image of your current location, or touch the **Hybrid** button to see street names and satellite images together.

3. Zoom in on the satellite images to see incredible detail of your current location. For many locations, you can zoom so close that you can look in your own backyard! Don't worry, though, they aren't live images.

QUICK**FACTS**

USING LOCATION SERVICES WITH YOUR DEVICE

Your device can approximate your current location through the use of Location Services. Location Services uses your cellular network (iPhone only), Wi-Fi network (iPhone and iPod touch), and global positioning system (GPS) (again, iPhone only) to find where you are. Location Services can also be used with other applications, like Camera, to provide location-specific information. You can turn Location Services on and off from within the General section of the Settings app. If Location Services is turned off, you will be asked to turn it on for apps that need its help.

BOOKMARK A LOCATION

You can create bookmarks for frequently viewed locations, much like bookmarking Web sites that you frequently browse.

1. Once you have a location, drop a pin on it.

2. Tap the pin to reveal the location's name.

3. Touch the **blue circle containing the arrow** to see information about the location.

4. Select the **Add To Bookmarks** button in the lower-right corner of the screen.

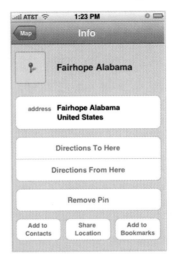

5. Enter the name of your bookmark, and tap the **Save** button.

To access a bookmarked location, tap the bookmark icon on the right side of the search field, and then tap the location in the Bookmarks screen.

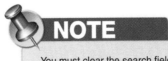

NOTE

You must clear the search field by tapping the **X** icon before the bookmark icon will be made available.

QUICKSTEPS

FINDING YOUR CURRENT LOCATION

You can find and track your current location using Location Services. Your approximate position is indicated by a blue circle, which can become larger or smaller, depending on the accuracy of information given to Location Services. Your movements are even tracked on the map as you go.

1. Tap the **locator** button in the lower-left corner of the Maps screen.

2. Location Services will use all the information at its disposal to approximate your location. The more accurate the information, the more precise Location Services can be.

3. If you have to drag your map and can no longer see your position on it, just tap the **locator** button again to zip the map back to your location.

GET DIRECTIONS TO AND FROM A LOCATION

Don't you just love having to fight the old paper maps while struggling to stay on the road? Who hasn't wadded up a paper map in frustration after having tried to fold it back? Maps to the rescue!

1. Tap the **Directions** button at the bottom of the Maps screen.

2. Enter starting and ending locations in the proper fields. Tap the field to bring up the keyboard.

3. Touch the **Route** button once the address information has been entered.

4. Maps brings up directions from your starting location to the ending location and displays the distance between them. Tap the **car**, **bus**, or **person** button at the top of the screen to see an estimate of how long it will take to get to the ending location by car, transit, or walking.

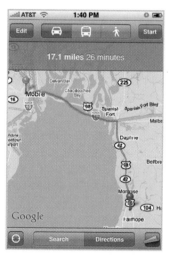

5. Tap the **Edit** button to modify your locations, if necessary.

6. Tap the **Start** button in the upper-right corner to begin following the directions.

7. Follow the directions step by step until you reach your destination, tapping the **left** or **right** arrow in the upper-right corner to move to the previous or next instruction.

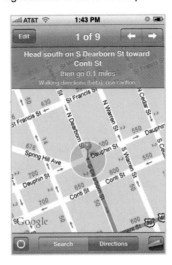

SEE LOCAL TRAFFIC CONDITIONS

I love the fact that Maps will even show you traffic conditions for your local area, although not all areas have this capability yet. You can use your device to see where traffic is moving along at a good clip or has slowed to a crawl.

1. Open a map to your current location.

2. Tap the **page** button in the lower-right corner.

3. Touch the **Show Traffic** button.

4. The map will now display roads in different colors (Figure 8-2), depending on the approximate rate of speed that the traffic is moving.

- Green shows traffic that is moving faster than 50 miles per hour.
- Yellow means traffic is moving between 25 and 50 miles per hour.
- Red displays when traffic is going slower than 25 miles per hour.
- Gray means that no data is currently available.

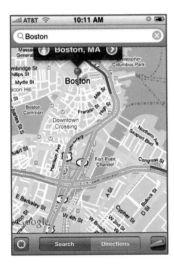

Figure 8-2: *Check traffic conditions based on the colors of roads.*

QUICKSTEPS

FINDING A LOCAL BUSINESS

You're really in need of a pizza fix, but you're in a section of town you're unfamiliar with or in a new city altogether. What to do? Whip out your iPhone or iPod touch and open Maps, and I'll show you how to find local businesses.

1. Enter a location for the business, such as the city you're in (the more precise, the better).

2. Enter a business name or type in the search field, and then tap the **Search** button in the lower-right corner.

3. Maps will display a map showing pins for all the locations it finds.

4. Tap a pin to see its name.

5. Tap the **blue circle containing the arrow** to see more detailed information about the business.

6. Use the information to contact the business. For example, tap the phone number to have iPhone call the business, or tap a URL to open the Web page for the particular business. You can even get directions to the business!

Add It All Up with Calculator

Calculator works exactly as advertised. If you're familiar with using a standard calculator, you'll be up and running instantly when you open the Calculator app. The keys in Calculator function exactly like those on the adding machine on your desk.

- *C* clears the number currently displayed.
- *MC* clears the data in memory.
- *M+* adds the number on the display to the number already in memory.
- *M-* subtracts the number on the display from the number already in memory.
- *MR* replaces the number currently on the display with the number already in memory.

Need something a bit more powerful than the standard calculator? You're in luck, because if you rotate your device to landscape, your standard calculator transforms into a state-of-the-art scientific calculator, with all the bells and whistles.

NOTE

The iPod touch must have wireless Internet access to view YouTube videos.

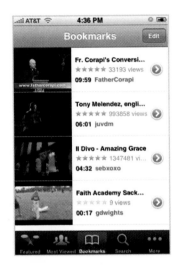

Watch Videos with YouTube

As I often like to say, "All work and no play make Dwight a dull boy" (apologies to Stephen King), so I'm thankful Apple threw in a little entertainment in the form of a YouTube application with the iPhone and iPod touch. Most videos that you can watch on the YouTube web site can be viewed on your iPhone or iPod touch.

1. Tap the **YouTube** icon on the Home screen to open it.
2. Several buttons at the bottom of the screen can help you find videos.
   - **Featured** contains videos that are being recognized by the YouTube staff.
   - **Most Viewed** shows you the most watched YouTube videos for the current day, current week, and all time.
   - **Bookmarks** lists your favorite videos that you bookmarked when you viewed them.
   - **Search** allows you to type information into the search field. YouTube finds all the videos that match the information you entered. Tap a video in the list to view it.
   - The **More** button gives you access to the most recent videos uploaded to YouTube, the top rated videos on YouTube, and a history of the videos you've watched.
3. Tap a video found in any of the buttons to watch it.
4. Use the playback controls on the screen to play, pause, fast-forward, or rewind the currently playing video. You can also e-mail a link for the video to a friend by tapping the **envelope** icon on the right side of the controls, bookmark the video by touching the **bookmark** icon on the left of the controls, and adjust the volume by dragging the slider at the bottom of the controls.

5. Tap the **Done** button in the upper-left corner of the screen when you're finished viewing it.

Apps that Keep You Productive

It's never a bad thing to stay on top of important information, and the iPhone and iPod touch are more than happy to help you do so. Three apps in particular can help you keep abreast of your finances, appointments, and your contacts.

Keep Up (and Down) with Your Stocks

If you own stock in a company, it's nice to be able to keep tabs on its performance throughout your busy day. The iPhone and iPod touch both provide you with the Stocks app, which allows for instant access to the latest stock quotes.

1. Open the Stocks app by tapping its icon on the Home screen.

2. Add a stock to your list.

   a. Tap the **information** button (*i*) at the lower-right corner of the screen.

   b. Touch the **+** button in the upper-left corner of the screen.

   c. Enter the company name or stock ID into the search field, and tap the **Search** button.

   d. Touch the name of the company you want to add to the stocks list, and it will appear in the Stocks screen.

3. Manage the stocks in your Stocks screen.

   - Rearrange the placement of stocks in the list by dragging the **three bars** on the right side of their name.

   - Remove a stock from the list by tapping the **red circle** to the left of its name and then tapping the **Delete** button that appears on its right.

   - When finished managing the stocks list, tap the **Done** button in the upper-right corner.

4. Touch the name of a stock in the main screen to see its individual performance over a given amount of time. Adjust the time by tapping the **1d**, **1w**, **1m**, **3m**, **6m**, **1y**, or **2y** button above the graph.

5. For more detailed information on the stock, tap the **Yahoo!** icon in the lower-left corner of the screen.

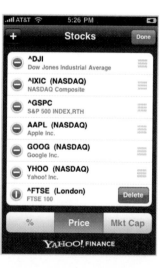

Track Appointments with Calendar

Calendar helps you keep on top of appointments you've already made, alerts you when an appointment is upcoming, lets you create new appointments (or events), and more. If you have a busy schedule, Calendar will quickly become a good friend.

1. Open Calendar by tapping its icon on the Home screen.

2. You are presented with a calendar displaying the current date.

3. Change your view of the calendar if you like by using the **List**, **Day**, or **Month** button at the bottom of the screen. Zoom to today's schedule from any calendar by tapping the **Today** button in the lower-left corner.

4. Tap a date in the calendar to see the events scheduled for that day.

5. Touch an event in the event list to see information about it. Tap the **Edit** button in the Event window if you want to modify its settings or delete the event altogether, and tap the **Done** button in the upper-right corner when finished.

6. Add a new event by tapping the + button in the upper-right corner of the Calendars screen.

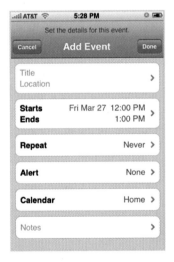

a. Enter the title and location of the event. Enter a start and end time for the event.

b. Decide whether the event repeats itself in the future.

c. Set alerts to remind you of the event.

d. Determine which calendar the event should belong to (if you use multiple
calendars, such as one for work and one for home).

e. Finally, enter any notes that might help you remember something about the event.

f. Tap **Done** when finished.

Manage Contacts

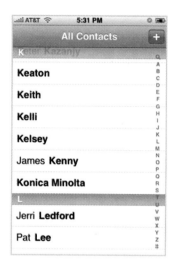

The iPhone and the iPod touch both come with the Contacts app, which helps
you manage your list of contacts in one place. We've covered adding and
syncing contacts in other chapters, so I'll just give you a quick peek at what
Contacts can do for you.

1. Tap the **Contacts** icon on the Home screen to launch the app.

2. You are presented with a list of your contacts, arranged in alphabetical order. Scroll
through the list by flicking or dragging your finger up or down the screen.

3. Tap a contact to see related information.

4. When viewing the information, tap the **Edit** button to make changes or additions to it.
You can also remove the contact from the list by tapping the **Delete Contact** button
and then tapping the **Delete Contact** confirmation button.

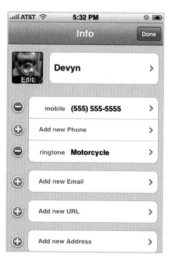

SEARCHING FOR ITEMS ON YOUR DEVICE

Your iPhone or iPod touch contains lots of information, applications, contacts, and other goodies. When you need to find something in a hurry, it can be a little daunting to hunt and peck through the items on your device. Spotlight allows you to search your entire device from one location. It can find applications on your device, as well as items contained in Contacts, Mail, Calendar, iPod, Music, and Notes.

1. Navigate to the main Home screen page, if you're not there already.

2. Flick your finger on the touchscreen from left to right to open Spotlight.

3. Use the keyboard to type the name of the item you are searching for, and tap the **Search** button in the lower-right corner of the screen.

4. The results will display on the screen. Flick up and down the screen to view all the search results, or tap a result to open it.

Create Reminders with Voice Memos

We've all had those moments when we thought of this mind-blowing, earth-shattering, life-affirming, never-before-thought-of idea that would bring peace to the world or have some other noble outcome, only to lose it when we discover we have no way to jot it down. But now, thanks to your iPhone or iPod touch, the world will no longer be the worse for you having forgotten these groundbreaking thoughts; you can record them using Voice Memos.

1. Tap the **Voice Memos** icon on the Home screen to launch the app (I love the old-style microphone).

2. Touch the **Record** button in the lower-left corner of the screen to begin recording your memo.

3. When finished, touch the **Stop** button on the lower-right side of the screen.

4. View your recorded memos by tapping the **List** button in the lower-right corner of the main screen (it looks like three bars stacked on top of one another).

5. Tap the **Play** button to the immediate left of a memo to listen to it.

6. E-mail the voice memo by tapping the **Share** button in the lower-left corner of the screen and then tapping the **E-mail Voice Memo** button.

How to...

- *Saving Battery Life by Enabling Airplane Mode*
- *Utilize Airplane Mode (iPhone Only)*
- *Modify Wi-Fi Settings*
- *Ending Annoying Network Requests*
- *Configure VPN Connections*
- *Select Alternate Cellular Carriers (iPhone Only)*
- *View Notifications*
- *Set Up Sounds (iPhone Only)*
- *Adjust Brightness*
- *Change Wallpaper (iPhone Only)*
- *Finding Cool Wallpaper on the Web*
- *Configure General Settings*
- *Using Multiple-Language Keyboards*
- *Modify Mail, Contacts, and Calendars*
- *Adjust Phone Settings (iPhone Only)*
- *Modify Safari*
- *Customize Receiving Messages*
- *Personalize iPod (iPhone) or Music and Video (iPod touch)*
- *Watching iPhone/iPod touch Videos On Your Television*
- *View Slideshows of Photos*
- *Sign In to the iTunes Store*

Chapter 9
Modifying Settings

Your iPhone or iPod touch was pretty great right out of the box, but it can be better. No, I'm not knocking Apple; in fact, I'm complimenting them. They saw the need for iPhone and iPod touch users to modify settings and make customizations. This chapter is all about those settings—those little tweaks that help you make an iPhone or iPod touch truly yours, as well as those preferences that are essential to the proper function of your device.

Communication and Customization

You can make many customizations to your iPhone or iPod touch, such as changing the ringtone and wallpaper. You also may need to adjust communication settings depending on your network and environment.

9

NOTE

All of the options in this chapter can be found within the Settings app of your iPhone or iPod touch.

QUICKFACTS

SAVING BATTERY LIFE BY ENABLING AIRPLANE MODE

When you enable Airplane Mode, you will inevitably use less power from your battery. This is great, especially if you are on a long flight, or if your battery is low and you only want to use the multimedia functions of your iPhone.

Utilize Airplane Mode (iPhone Only)

When you fly, you must turn off your cell phone to prevent it from interfering with the radio transmissions of the airplane. Well, if you do that, you won't have access to your media files, such as movies and music, will you? On most phones, you would be right, but the iPhone includes a great feature called Airplane Mode. Airplane Mode disables functions of your iPhone that use radio waves (Bluetooth, Wi-Fi, and cellular communications), but still allows you to use the other apps. You won't be able to make or receive calls or use the Internet, but at least you can watch your movies and listen to your tunes.

To enable or disable Airplane Mode:

1. Tap the Settings icon on the Home screen.

2. Touch the **On/Off** toggle switch to enable or disable Airplane Mode.

Modify Wi-Fi Settings

The Wi-Fi settings help you enable the Wi-Fi capabilities of your device and choose a wireless network to connect to.

1. Tap the Settings icon on the Home screen.

2. Select the **Wi-Fi** button.

3. Enable or disable Wi-Fi by tapping the **On/Off** toggle switch.

4. Tap the network you want to join, if it appears in the list.

5. Enter the network's password, if one is required.

6. If the network you want to join doesn't show up in the list, tap the **Other** button.

7. Enter the network name.

8. Tap the **Security** button to select the type of security used by the network (if any), and then tap the **Other Network** button in the upper-left corner to return to the Other Network screen.

9. Enter the password needed for the network.

10. Tap the **Join** button in the lower-right corner.

11. Once you're connected to the network, the Wi-Fi icon will display in the upper-left corner of your screen.

You can view connection information (such as your device's IP address) and make modifications to your device's settings (like proxy settings and renew IP address leases) for the network you're connected to.

1. In the Wi-Fi Networks screen, tap the **blue circle containing the arrow** located to the right of the name for the network to which you're connected, in order to view the settings and options available.

2. Tap the **Forget This Network** button if you want the device to no longer automatically log in to the network when it is discovered.

3. Press the **DHCP**, **BootP**, or **Static** button to see your device's IP address information.

4. Touch the **Renew Lease** button to have your device request a new IP address from the network's router or server, if using DHCP or BootP. You may want to give this a try if you are having difficulty accessing the Internet.

5. Set the HTTP proxy, if your network requires it. This is something you'll definitely need to check with your network administrator about.

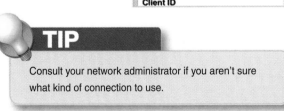

TIP

Consult your network administrator if you aren't sure what kind of connection to use.

ENDING ANNOYING NETWORK REQUESTS

As the proud owner of an iPhone or iPod touch, if you have Wi-Fi enabled, it's only a matter of time before you notice that your device frequently asks if you want to join a network it has discovered. This can get a tad annoying after a while, especially if you live in a heavily populated area where many people may have wireless routers. To end these bothersome inquiries:

1. Tap the **Settings** icon on the Home screen.

2. Select the **Wi-Fi** button.

3. Tap the **On/Off** toggle switch next to Ask To Join Networks.

Ask to Join Networks ON

Configure VPN Connections

The VPN button will only appear when you have configured VPN in the Network section of the General settings, which we'll learn more about later in this chapter. Tap the **On/Off** toggle switch to enable or disable the VPN connection.

Select Alternate Cellular Carriers (iPhone Only)

The Carrier settings will appear in the Settings app only if you are outside of your carrier's network. When you're outside your carrier's network, you will see "No service" appear in the upper-left corner of your iPhone's screen, and you won't be able to make calls, receive visual voicemail, or access the Internet via the cellular network.

If you are outside your normal carrier's network, tap the **Carrier** button to see other networks that may be available. If other networks are available, they must have a contract with your current carrier in order for you to make calls.

CAUTION

Roaming charges may apply! If you use this service, don't be surprised if they have to deliver your cellular bill on a flatbed truck.

TIP

Turning off notifications can help preserve your battery life.

View Notifications

Notifications only shows up in Settings if you've installed an application that uses the Apple Push Notification service. Push notifications let you know when new information is available for an app, even if that app isn't currently running. Notifications allows you to enable or disable notifications for these apps either altogether or for individual notification types.

1. Tap the Settings icon on the Home screen.

2. Touch the **Notifications** button.

3. To enable or disable notifications, touch the **On/Off** toggle switch.

Push ON

4. For accounts that use Fetch, select a time interval for the device to look for new information.

Set Up Sounds (iPhone Only)

I'll bet you can't guess which options the Sounds settings control! From here, you can determine which ringtone to use; whether your phone should vibrate or not when you receive a call, e-mail, or text message; and more.

1. Touch the **Settings** icon on the Home screen.

2. Select the **Sounds** button to see the available options.

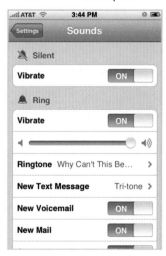

NOTE

Whenever the Ring/Silent switch on the left side of your iPhone is set to Silent, you will no longer be able to hear the phone ringing, any alert notifications, or sound effects. The only items that you will be able to hear are alarms you've set in the Clock app.

3. Under the Silent section, touch the **On/Off** toggle switch for Vibrate to have the iPhone vibrate when you receive a call or other form of communication when the Silent/Ring switch is set to Silent.

4. Toggle the **On/Off** switch for the Vibrate option under the Ring section to have the iPhone vibrate and ring when you receive a call.

5. Drag the **volume** slider to adjust the volume of your ringer.

6. Tap the **Ringtone** button to select a ringtone. Tap the **Sounds** button in the upper-left corner to return to the Sounds screen.

7. Choose an alert for new text messages by tapping the **New Text Message** button and selecting an alarm from the list. Tap the **Sounds** button in the upper-left corner to return to the Sounds screen.

8. Toggle the **On/Off** switch for the following items to enable or disable alerts for them:

- New Voicemail
- New Mail
- Sent Mail
- Calendar Alerts
- Lock Sounds
- Keyboard Clicks

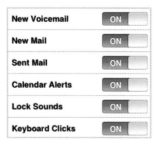

Adjust Brightness

You can manually adjust the brightness of your device's screen, or allow the device to automatically adjust the brightness, depending on the lighting conditions where you are using it.

1. Open the Settings app by touching its icon on the Home screen.

2. Tap the **Brightness** button to view the available options.

3. Drag the slider to manually adjust the screen brightness.

4. Toggle the **Auto-Brightness On/Off** switch to allow the device to automatically adjust the brightness.

Change Wallpaper (iPhone Only)

Whenever you unlock your iPhone, you will see a wallpaper picture. You can set that wallpaper here.

1. Open Settings by tapping its icon on the Home screen.

2. Tap the **Wallpaper** button.

3. Select the album that contains the picture you want to use for your wallpaper.

4. Touch the picture you want to use for wallpaper to open it full-screen.

5. Move and/or resize the image as needed by dragging your fingers on the screen.

6. Tap the **Set Wallpaper** button to begin using the image.

QUICKFACTS

FINDING COOL WALLPAPER ON THE WEB

The wallpaper that comes with your device is nice, but only just enough to whet the appetite. In addition to using your own photos as wallpaper, you can download wallpaper for the iPhone or iPod touch from hundreds of sites on the World Wide Web. Simply go to Google (www.google.com) and type iPhone wallpaper in the search field and then click the **Search** button. The last time I did this, I was rewarded with 12,100,000 hits! A word of caution, though: All of these sites may not be family-friendly.

Configure General Settings

The General settings allow you to view information about your device and adjust communication and security settings. You can also restore your device to its original state.

1. Open the Settings app by tapping its icon on the Home screen.

2. Select the **General** button.

3. Tap the **About** button to see vital information about your device, such as the capacity available, the version of software it's running, the serial and model numbers, Wi-Fi and Bluetooth addresses, and more. Tap the **General** button to return to the General screen.

4. Press the **Usage** button (iPhone only) to see how long it's been since you last fully charged your iPhone, the call time, and the amount of data you've sent and received over the cellular network. Tap the **General** button to return to the General screen.

5. Tap the **Wallpaper** button (iPod touch only), select a picture for your wallpaper, and tap the **Set Wallpaper** button.

6. Modify the communication settings by tapping the **Network** button.

- Toggle the **Enable 3G On/Off** switch (iPhone only) to enable or disable communication with 3G networks. Disabling 3G can also lighten the load on your battery.

- Toggling the **Data Roaming** switch (iPhone only) lets you turn data roaming on or off (off is the default). Turning Data Roaming on allows you to use the Internet on alternate carriers when you are outside your original carrier's network. Turning this feature on can also cost you quite a bundle of money, so use it judiciously.

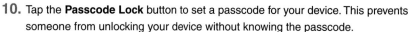

- If you use a virtual private network (VPN) to access a remote network, tap the **VPN** button, toggle the **VPN On/Off** switch to On, and enter the information for the VPN in the Add Configuration window as prescribed by your network administrator.

- The Wi-Fi button is a shortcut for the Wi-Fi Networks screen, which was discussed earlier in this chapter.

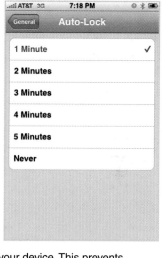

7. Tap the **Bluetooth** button (iPhone only), and then toggle the **Bluetooth On/Off** switch to On, enabling Bluetooth on your device. Bluetooth can be used to connect with other wireless devices that use the Bluetooth protocol, such as headphones.

8. Toggle the **Location Services On/Off** switch to enable or disable the services, which were discussed Chapter 8.

9. Your iPhone or iPod touch will lock itself automatically after a specified amount of time. Use the **Auto-Lock** button to set this time.

10. Tap the **Passcode Lock** button to set a passcode for your device. This prevents someone from unlocking your device without knowing the passcode.

   - Tap the **Passcode Lock** button.

   - Enter a four-digit passcode.

   - Re-enter the four-digit passcode for verification.

   - Use the settings in the Passcode Lock screen to modify its settings. Choose from the following options:

      - Turn Passcode Off

      - Change Passcode

      - Adjust how often the passcode is needed using the **Require Passcode** button.

      - Toggle the **Show SMS Preview** switch to show or not show previews of text messages you receive.

      - Toggle the **Erase Data** switch to enable or disable this security measure.

CAUTION

When using the Erase Data feature, all data on this device will be erased after 10 failed attempts at entering the passcode.

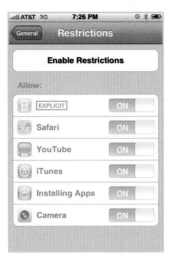

11. The Restrictions button lets you assign a passcode to certain applications on your device, preventing anyone who doesn't know the passcode from using them. This is great for keeping your kids from viewing Internet content that may not be family-friendly.

- Tap the **Restrictions** button.
- Touch the **Enable Restrictions** button.
- Enter a passcode, and then re-enter it.
- Toggle the **On/Off** switch for each of the apps listed to enable or disable the passcode for it.

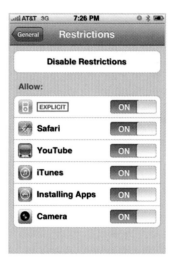

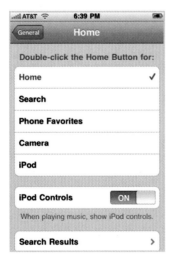

12. The Home Button option (iPhone only) lets you change what happens when you double-click the **Home** button.

- Decide whether double-clicking the Home button takes you to the Home screen, Phone Favorites, or opens the iPod app.
- Toggle the **iPod Controls On/Off** switch to show the iPod controls while a song is playing when you double-click the Home button.

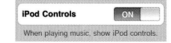

13. Select the **Date & Time** button to adjust the date and time settings for your device.

- iPhone only:

    1. Toggle the **Set Automatically On/Off** switch (iPhone only) to On to sync the time with your cellular network. The time is even updated when you move to another time zone. This feature may be dependent on your cellular carrier.

    2. Toggle the **Set Automatically On/Off** switch (iPhone only) to Off to manually set the date and time.

  a. Select the **Time Zone** button, and enter the name of a major city that's in your time zone using the keyboard.

  b. Touch the **Date & Time** button in the upper-left corner to return to the Date & Time screen.

  c. Tap the **Set Date & Time** button to enter the date and time.

  d. Touch the **date** field to adjust the month, day, and year.

  e. Touch the **time** field to change the time (don't forget to set A.M. or P.M.).

- iPod touch:

    1. Tap the **Time Zone** button, and enter the name of a major city that's in your time zone.

    2. Touch the **Date & Time** button in the upper-left corner, and then tap the **Set Date & Time** button to enter the date and time.

    3. Touch the **date** field to adjust the month, day, and year.

    4. Touch the **time** field to change the time (don't forget to set A.M. or P.M.).

14. The Keyboard button lets you set various options for typing with the touchscreen keyboard.

- Toggle the **On/Off** switch to enable or disable each of the four options: Auto-Correction, Auto-Capitalization, Enable Caps Lock, and "." Shortcut (which will insert a period followed by a space when you double-tap the **SPACEBAR**).

• Tap the **International Keyboards** button to enable keyboards for different languages.

15. The International button lets you make language- and region-specific modifications to your device.

- • Tap the **Language** button to select a default language for your device.

- • The Keyboards button lets you enable multiple-language keyboards (see step 14 and the "Using Multiple-Language Keyboards" QuickFacts for more information).

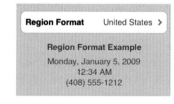

- • Use the **Region Format** button to choose the format for displaying items like the date, time, and phone numbers.

16. The Reset button helps you set multiple settings back to their defaults. When you tap the Reset button, you can see the various options available. To execute each option, tap its button, and then confirm or cancel the action (Figure 9-1).

- • Reset All Settings does just what it says. All preferences and settings you've made on your device are reset. Don't worry: Your information and media will not be deleted.

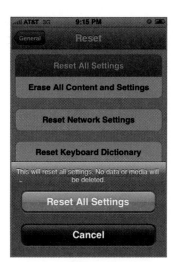

Figure 9-1: *Tap the red button to confirm the action, or press Cancel if you're not so sure.*

CAUTION

Stay away from the Erase All Content And Settings button if you don't intend to do just that! You will lose any information or data that you haven't backed up.

NOTE

Many of Mail's options have been discussed in Chapter 4, so there will only be a brief explanation of them here.

- Erase All Content And Settings resets all of your device's settings to their defaults and erases all information and media from it. You cannot use your device while the content and settings are being reset (this process could take a long time).

- When you reject words suggested by your device while using the keyboard, you are adding the words you used to the keyboard dictionary. Tap the **Reset Keyboard Dictionary** button to clear the words you've added to the dictionary.

- Reset Network Settings erases all information about networks you've joined and any VPNs you've logged into.

- When you have lots of apps installed, the icons on your main Home screen can get all discombobulated. Reset the main Home screen layout by tapping the **Reset Home Screen Layout** button.

- Some applications ask if they can use Location Services to locate where you are. These requests are called location warnings, and your app stops asking the second time you confirm it's OK to use your current location. You can have the app resume location warnings by tapping the **Reset Location Warnings** button.

Application Settings

Several applications on your device also have settings that you can configure to customize your user experience. Some third-party applications may also allow you to customize settings, and the Settings app is where those configurations can be applied.

Modify Mail, Contacts, and Calendars

Items in the Mail, Contacts, Calendars button allow you to set up and make modifications to your e-mail accounts, alter how your contacts are displayed, and customize the Calendar app's functions.

1. Open the Settings app by tapping its icon in the Home screen.

2. Select the **Mail, Contacts, Calendars** button.

3. The Accounts section of the Mail, Contacts, Calendars screen lists the accounts you've added.

- Tap an account to view and modify its settings.

These settings can be different, depending on your e-mail provider, and you won't even have an Advanced button if you have a MobileMe account.

NOTE

- Enable or disable the account by toggling the **Account On/Off** switch.

- Tap any of the fields to make changes to its settings.

- Change the default SMTP server for the account using the **SMTP** button.

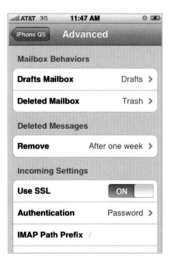

- Tap the **Advanced** button to alter how the account handles draft and deleted e-mails, as well as security settings.

- Select the **Delete Account** button to remove the account from your device.

4. The Fetch New Data button is discussed in Chapter 4.

5. The Mail section allows you to make adjustments to how Mail displays your e-mails, have it ask for confirmation before deleting e-mails, set a signature for outgoing e-mail, and more.

- The Show button lets you determine how many e-mails will be listed in the Mail app.

NOTE

Be aware that the signature will appear at the bottom of every e-mail you send. If you choose to use a silly quote as your signature, you might want to think twice if you use your device for business purposes.

- Tap the **Preview** button to set how many lines of the message will be displayed when viewing the message list.

- Choose a size for fonts in the Mail app by using the **Minimum Font Size** button.

- Decide whether the To/Cc field shows in the message list by toggling the **Show To/Cc Label On/Off** switch.

- If you want to be asked for confirmation each time you delete an e-mail, toggle the **Ask Before Deleting On/Off** switch to On.

- Toggle the **Load Remote Images On/Off** switch to automatically download images in e-mails formatted with HTML or not.

- You can stealthily copy yourself on any e-mail you send by enabling the **Always Bcc Myself** option. Just toggle the **On/Off** switch to On.

- Create an e-mail signature using the **Signature** button. Use the keyboard to enter any signature you want.

- Set the e-mail account that your device will use as its default using the **Default Account** button. This is the account that will be used when you send an e-mail from an app outside of Mail, like when you e-mail a picture from the Photos app.

6. The Contacts section of the Mail, Contacts, Calendars screen lets you use the Sort Order and Display Order buttons to decide which method of order better suits your tastes.

7. The Import SIM Contacts button (iPhone only) in the Contacts section allows you to sync contacts that are stored on your iPhone's SIM card.

8. Finally, let's take a look at the options under the Calendars section of the Mail, Contacts, Calendars screen.

- Have your device alert you when new meeting invitations are received by toggling the **New Invitation Alerts** switch to On.

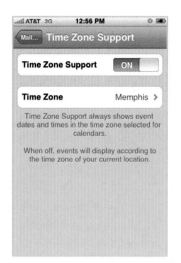

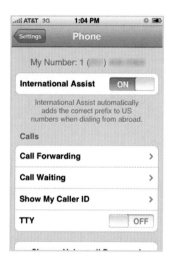

- If you are a MobileMe or Microsoft Exchange account user, you will have a Sync button that allows you to sync events at certain time intervals.

- The Time Zone Support button lets Calendar display event dates and times in the time zone of the city you choose. Tap the button to enable or disable Time Zone Support, and choose a city using the Time Zone button.

- Select a default calendar to use by tapping the **Default Calendar** button.

Adjust Phone Settings (iPhone Only)

The Phone settings let you configure how your Phone app handles calls, change your voicemail password (if you use one), assign a PIN to your SIM card, and use services offered by your cellular carrier.

1. Open the Settings app (I think you've got that part down by this point in the chapter).

2. Tap the **Phone** button to see its options. Your phone number is displayed at the top of the screen (this may be dependent on your cellular carrier).

3. Toggle the **International Assist On/Off** switch to enable or disable this feature, which automatically adds the correct prefix to a number in the United States that you dial while abroad.

4. The Calls section of the Phone screen helps you set up call forwarding, call waiting, and more.

   a. Tap the **Call Forwarding** button to view its screen.

      - Toggle the **Call Forwarding On/Off** switch to enable or disable the feature.

      - Tap the **Forwarding To** button to enter a number that you want your calls to be forwarded to.

   b. Enable or disable your iPhone's call-waiting feature by toggling the **On/Off** switch found on the Call Waiting screen.

NOTE

If you disable call waiting and someone calls you when you are already on another call, the second call will be sent directly to voicemail.

c. If you're someone who likes to remain anonymous, toggle the **Show My Caller ID** switch to Off, which prevents people you are calling from seeing your name and number on their phone.

d. Your iPhone will work with Teletype (TTY) machines, which are devices used by deaf or hearing-impaired persons to communicate by typing and reading. To enable this functionality on your iPhone, you will need to toggle the **TTY** switch to On and connect a TTY machine to it using the iPhone TTY Adapter cable, which is available at www.apple.com/store.

5. For a bit more security, you can assign a password to your voicemail, which prevents anyone who doesn't know the password from hearing your personal voicemail messages.

    a. Tap the **Change Voicemail Password** button.

    b. Enter your current voicemail password (if you have one already set up), and tap the **Done** button in the upper-right corner. If you haven't set up a password before, just tap the **Done** button in the upper-right corner.

    c. Enter a new voicemail password, and tap the **Done** button in the upper-right corner. The next time you check your voicemail, you will be prompted to enter your password.

6. Another security feature included here is the ability to lock your SIM card with a PIN (personal identification number). Your cellular carrier may require you to use a SIM PIN.

    a. Tap the **SIM PIN** button.

    b. Toggle the **SIM PIN** switch to On.

    c. Enter a PIN for your SIM using the onscreen keypad.

    d. You will be required to enter your SIM PIN each time you turn on your iPhone.

CAUTION

If you incorrectly enter the PIN after three tries, your SIM card will be disabled, and you will need to contact your cellular carrier for help in getting it re-enabled.

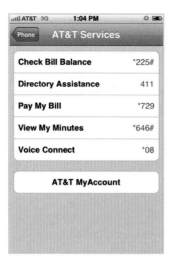

7. Some carriers provide easy ways for you to access the features they offer to customers, such as numbers to quickly access information about their accounts. For example, those iPhone users in the United States will see an AT&T Services button at the bottom of their Phone screen. When we tap that button, we have access to many services offered to AT&T customers.

Modify Safari

Safari, the Web browser built in to your iPhone or iPod touch, allows you to customize your Web surfing experience to some degree.

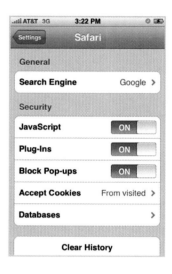

1. Open the Settings app.

2. Tap the **Safari** button to see available options.

3. The Search Engine button allows you to change the default search engine for Safari.

   a. Tap the **Search Engine** button.

   b. Touch the **Google** or **Yahoo!** button to use one of them as Safari's default.

   c. Press the **Safari** button in the upper-left corner to return to the Safari screen.

4. Turn on **AutoFill** if you want to have Safari enter your name, address information, and passwords automatically for websites that support such things.

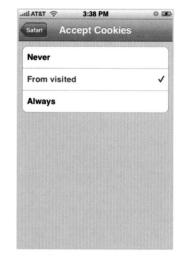

5. Enable or disable JavaScript, plug-ins that increase functionality, or blocking of pop-ups while surfing by toggling the **On/Off** switches for JavaScript, Plug-Ins, and Block Pop-ups.

6. Tap the **Accept Cookies** button to decide to never accept cookies, accept cookies only from sites you've visited, or always accept all cookies.

7. You can clear your browsing history, the cookies you've accepted, and Safari's cache by tapping the appropriate button: **Clear History**, **Clear Cookies**, and **Clear Cache**, respectively.

NOTE

If you're not a developer, I'd advise leaving the Debug Console off.

8. Some web applications can store information on your device. Tap the **Databases** button to see which apps store this information, as well as how much space is being used for the database.

9. The **Developer** button gives you the option to enable or disable the Debug Console by toggling its **On/Off** switch.

Customize Receiving Messages

These settings let you determine whether to view previews of new incoming text messages and whether the preview should repeat if you don't respond to the first alert.

1. Open the Settings app.

2. Tap the **Messages** button to see available options.

3. Toggle the **On/Off** switches for Show Preview and Repeat Alert, according to your preference.

Personalize iPod (iPhone) or Music and Video (iPod touch)

Use these settings to modify playback for your music and videos.

1. Open the Settings app.

2. Tap the **iPod** button to view its options.

3. Toggle the **On/Off** switch for Shake To Shuffle to On to allow you to change the song currently playing by simply shaking your device.

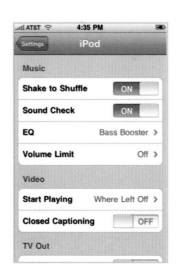

4. Sound Check is a feature of iTunes that adjusts the volume of all files so that they will play back at a relatively similar sound level. To use this feature, it must be enabled in iTunes, and then you must turn the feature on in the iPod features.

   a. Enable Sound Check in iTunes.

   • In iTunes for Mac, select **Preferences** from the iTunes menu, click the **Playback** tab, and select the **Sound Check** check box.

NOTE

The iPod screen contains three sections: Music, Video, and TV Out. The iPod touch does things a bit differently; there is no iPod button under Settings. Instead, the iPod touch separates the items found in the Music section of the iPhone's iPod button into a Music button under Settings, and the items found in the Video and TV Out sections into a Video button. The settings are the same, but are located under different buttons.

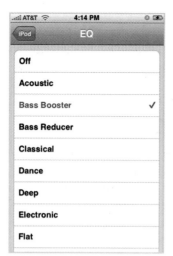

- In iTunes for PC, select **Preferences** from the Edit menu, click the **Playback** tab, and select the **Sound Check** check box.

b. Enable or disable Sound Check on your device by toggling its **On/Off** switch.

5. The EQ button lets you choose from a list of preconfigured equalizers. These equalizers can optimize the sound to accommodate different styles of music.

6. In some cases, it may be prudent to limit the level at which the volume can be set.

a. Tap the **Volume Limit** button to set a volume limit using the slider.

NOTE

If you don't know whether to use NTSC or PAL, consult the documentation that came with your television.

b. Tap the **Lock Volume Limit** button to add a passcode to this feature.

7. The Start Playing button lets you tell your device where to begin playback of a video: from the beginning of the video or from where you left off the last time you viewed it.

8. Enable or disable the Closed Captioning feature using the **On/Off** toggle switch.

9. Enable widescreen viewing of your videos when watching them on your television by toggling the **Widescreen** switch to On.

10. If you wish to connect your device to a television to play video, you can watch it in widescreen format by toggling the **Widescreen On/Off** switch.

11. To play video on your television, your iPhone or iPod touch needs to broadcast using a standard the television understands. Tap the **TV Signal** button to select the NTSC or PAL standard.

WATCHING iPHONE/iPOD TOUCH VIDEOS ON YOUR TELEVISION

Did you know you could watch videos from your iPhone or iPod touch on your television? It's a pretty cool feature, but you can enjoy this experience only if you have the proper cabling. You can use the Apple Component AV Cable, the Apple Composite AV Cable, or another compatible cable. You can buy the Apple cables from www.apple.com/store.

View Slideshows of Photos

The Photos button allows you to adjust how slideshows play on your device.

1. Open the Settings app.

2. Tap the **Photos** button to see your slideshow options.

3. Determine how long each slide is displayed using the **Play Each Slide For** button.

4. Choose from one of five cool transitions by touching the **Transition** button and tapping the one you like best.

5. Cause your slideshow to repeat by toggling the **Repeat** switch to On.

6. You can randomly view slides by toggling the **Shuffle** switch to On.

Sign In to the iTunes Store

The Store button allows you to sign in to your iTunes Store account, and even view details of the account, from your iPhone or iPod touch.

1. Open the Settings app.

2. Tap the **Store** button to sign in or out of your account, or to view details of your account.

How to...

- Find Featured Applications
- Browse Categories for Applications
- *Using Paid or Free Apps?*
- Check Out the Top 25 Paid and Free Apps
- *Finding App Reviews Online*
- Search for Specific Applications
- Install a New App
- Update Currently Installed Applications
- Delete Apps from your Device
- Syncing Purchased or Downloaded Apps
- Understand the App Store Interface
- Easily Find the Latest and Greatest Apps
- Browsing to Quickly Find Specific Apps
- Submit Reviews of Your Favorite (and Not-So-Favorite) Apps
- Discover a Few of My Favorite Applications and Games
- *Jailbreaking the iPhone/iPod touch*

Chapter 10

Getting to Know the App Store

As you may know by now, applications are the lifeblood of your iPhone, and even more so with the iPod touch. While the apps that come with your device are great, to be sure, they most certainly do not cover the gamut of all that can be accomplished with it. Luckily, application developers have stepped in to fill the void, and are offering literally tens of thousands of apps that can do almost anything you can think of. Apple has provided the App Store as a means for those developers to get their product to you, and in this chapter we'll see how to use the App Store on both your device and within iTunes.

Use the App Store on Your iPhone 3G/iPod touch

The App Store on your iPhone or iPod touch may not look too complicated at first glance, but there's a lot of power in this seemingly small app. You can browse for applications in one of several different ways, see the most popular apps, download paid and free apps, and more.

Find Featured Applications

When you first launch the App Store, you are taken to the Featured screen, where you are treated to the latest and greatest apps available for your iPhone or iPod touch.

VIEWING THE NEWEST APPS

As new apps are added to the App Store, they appear here for your perusal.

1. Tap the **App Store** icon on the Home screen to open it.

2. You are automatically taken to the Featured screen.

3. Tap the **New** tab at the top to see a list of the newest applications.

4. Scroll through the list of apps by flicking your finger up and down on the screen.

5. When you find an app that interests you, tap its name to see its Info page, where you can read a description, and more. See the section called *Install a New App* later in this chapter for instructions on loading the app onto your device.

NOTE

The icon and name of the app show on the left side of the list, along with its rating, and its price appears on the right side.

VIEWING THE HOTTEST APPS

The apps that are generating lots of buzz are listed under the What's Hot section of the Featured screen.

1. Open the App Store by tapping its icon on the Home screen.

2. From within the Featured screen, tap the **What's Hot** tab.

3. Scroll through the list of apps by flicking your finger up and down on the screen.

4. When you find an app that interests you, tap its name to see its Info page, and read on to see if it's something you'd like to install. See the section called *Install a New App* later in this chapter for instructions on loading the app onto your device.

Browse Categories for Applications

The good folks who manage the App Store have seen fit to categorize applications, which can make it fairly simple to find an app that fits the topic you need.

1. Tap the **App Store** icon on the Home screen.

2. When App Store opens, tap the **Categories** button at the bottom of the screen.

3. Scroll through the list of categories by flicking your finger up or down on the touchscreen. Categories listed include:

- Games
- Entertainment
- Utilities
- Social Networking
- Music

- Productivity
- Lifestyle
- Reference
- Travel
- Sports

- Navigation
- Healthcare & Fitness
- News
- Photography
- Finance

- Business
- Education
- Weather
- Books
- Medical

4. Tap a category that interests you to see apps it contains.

5. Each category lists apps according to three subcategories:
   - Top Paid
   - Top Free
   - Release Date

6. Tap the subcategory you want to view and flick the screen up and down to scroll through the apps listed.

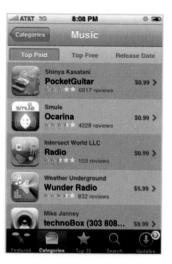

7. Touch the name of an app to see its Info page and deem its worthiness. See the section called *Install a New App* later in this chapter for instructions on loading the app onto your iPhone or iPod touch.

USING PAID OR FREE APPS?

To pay or not to pay? Well, that all depends on you and what your needs are. You will find thousands of apps, both free and paid, so there's bound to be something in both categories that piques your interest. Some apps even have *lite* versions, which are free versions that give you an idea of how the full version of the app works (sort of like a trial run). You may also notice that some free apps contain advertisements. If you need a state-of-the-art app that specializes in a given task, you may not have an alternative but to shell out some cash.

Check Out the Top 25 Paid and Free Apps

Apple keeps tabs on its best-selling, or most frequently downloaded apps, too. The App Store keeps up with the top 25 paid and free apps, and you can see even more by tapping the Top 50 button at the bottom of the screen.

1. Open the App Store.

2. Tap the **Top 25** button at the bottom of the screen.

3. To see the top 25 apps folks are forking over their hard-earned money for, tap the **Top Paid** tab at the top of the screen.

4. To see the 25 apps people are downloading at no cost, tap the **Top Free** tab at the top of the screen.

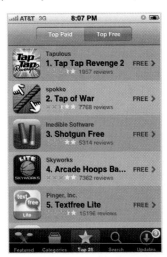

5. Tap an app to see its Info page. Read the section called *Install a New App* later in this chapter for instructions on loading the app onto your device.

Search for Specific Applications

Perhaps the easiest method to hasten your quest for that perfect app is to simply search for it.

1. Open the App Store.
2. Tap the **Search** button at the bottom of the screen.

3. Touch the **Search** field at the top of the screen and enter the title of the app (if you know it) or a few keywords.
4. The App Store lists apps that match your criteria as you type.

5. Tap the name of an app to view its Info screen, and see the next section called *Install a New App* for help with loading the app onto your device.

Install a New App

Finally, for the part you've all been patiently waiting for, it's time to install a new app on your iPhone or iPod touch.

1. Once you've found the app you want, scroll down the Info screen to see screenshots of the app in action. Tap a screenshot to view it full screen.

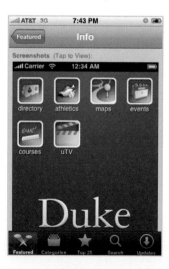

2. Tap the **Reviews** button to see what people are saying about the app.

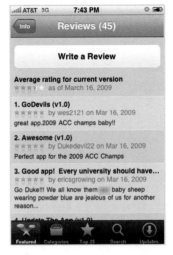

3. Scroll through the reviews to read them. If you've used this app before, tap the **Write a Review** button to submit your own thoughts on the app.

4. Touch the **Tell a Friend** button to send an email to someone telling him or her about the app.

5. Tap the **Report a Problem** button to submit an issue to the developer.

6. If you want to install the app on your device, tap the **price** button in the upper right corner of the Info screen (at the top of the page).

7. Tap the **Install** button in the upper right of the screen.

8. Enter your iTunes Store password when prompted, and then tap the **OK** button.

9. You will be rushed back to your Home screen where you will see the icon for your new app and a bar indicating its installation progress.

10. Once installation is complete you can launch your new app by tapping its icon.

Update Currently Installed Applications

Apps are frequently updated on the App Store, due to the developer resolving bugs, or to enhancing functionality. Sometimes an update to the iPhone or iPod touch's firmware can cause a conflict with an app, and an update is required to fix the incompatibility. Whatever the reasons, you will have to update most apps at some point. To perform these updates from the App Store:

1. Open the App Store.

2. Tap the **Updates** button at the bottom of the screen.

NOTE

Installation time will vary depending on the size of the app and the type of Internet connection you are using. For example, downloading an app will be much faster on a Wi-Fi network than using your cellular carrier's 3G network.

3. The App Store application will compare the versions of apps installed on your device with their current versions on the App Store. If the versions found on the App Store are newer than those on the device, the app will be listed in the Updates screen.

4. To install all of the upgrades, tap the **Update All** button in the upper right corner.

5. To upgrade individual apps:

   a. Tap the app you wish to upgrade to view the Update screen, which will usually describe what issues this upgrade resolves, or what functions have been tweaked.

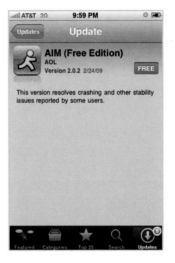

   b. Tap the **price** (or **Free**) button.

   c. Tap the **Install** button.

   d. Enter your iTunes password and tap **OK**.

6. The new version of your app will be installed.

Delete Apps from Your Device

Sometimes an app outlives its usefulness, or worse, didn't have any to begin with. If either is the case, it's time to free up some space on your device. Removing an app from your iPhone or iPod touch is remarkably simple.

1. Locate the icon of the doomed app on one of your Home screens.

2. Press and hold the **apps** icon until all icons on the screen begin to shake.

3. Apps that you've added to your device will appear with an X in the upper left corner of their icon.

4. To remove the app, tap the **X**.

5. Tap the **Delete** button when prompted to confirm the removal of the app.

6. Your device will ask you to rate the app before it completes the grisly task.

   a. Touch the number of stars you feel the app deserves (1 to 5 = worst to best).

   b. Tap the **Rate** button to submit your review.

   c. Tap **No Thanks** to decline the opportunity to offer your opinion of the app.

UICKSTEPS

SYNCING PURCHASED OR DOWNLOADED APPS

iTunes is a stickler for keeping things in sync, and it's no different when it comes to apps you've downloaded or purchased using the App Store on your device.

1. Connect your device to your computer.

2. Open iTunes.

3. Click the device's icon in the source list.

4. Select the **Applications** tab and choose a sync method (see Chapter 2 for more info).

5. Click **Apply** in the lower right, if necessary; otherwise, click **Sync**.

6. Any apps you downloaded are backed up into iTunes, and they are added to the Applications section of the source list.

Utilize the App Store within iTunes

The App Store in iTunes is, in my opinion, the best place to find new apps for your device, unless of course you are away from your computer. I love the iTunes App Store's interface and search tools, and it's faster to find apps on it than through the App Store on iPhone or iPod touch.

Understand the App Store Interface

The App Store's interface is designed with ease of use in mind. First we need to get to the App Store:

1. Open iTunes.

2. Select the iTunes Store from the Store section of the source list.

3. Click the **App Store** link under the iTunes Store category on the left side of the window to open the App Store.

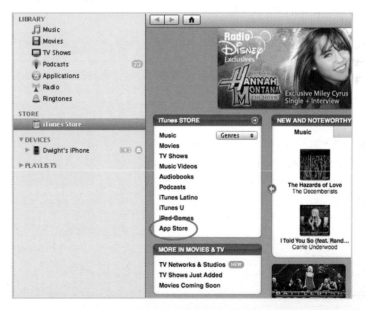

4. The App Store window is divided into sections that cover different categories:

- iTunes Store
- Categories
- More In Apps
- New and Noteworthy
- What's Hot
- Staff Favorites
- Quick Links
- Top Paid Apps
- Top Free Apps

5. Click any app icon to see the information page for the app.

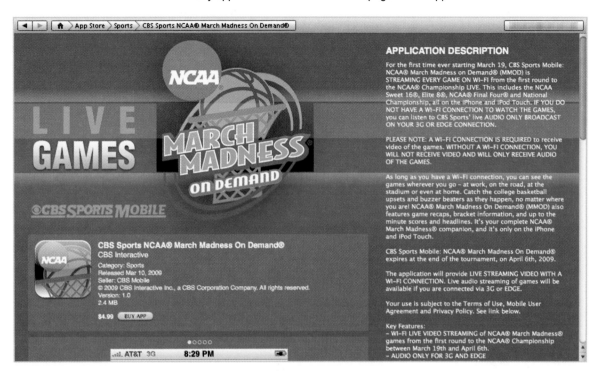

6. Click a link in the iTunes Store section to jump to another department of the iTunes Store.

7. Select a topic under Categories to see apps that fit certain criteria for the category.

8. Click the **App Store FAQs** link in the More in Apps section to see a list of the most frequently asked questions about the App Store.

9. The New and Noteworthy section lists the latest apps to hit the App Store. Figure 10-1 points out a few tools for navigating the section.

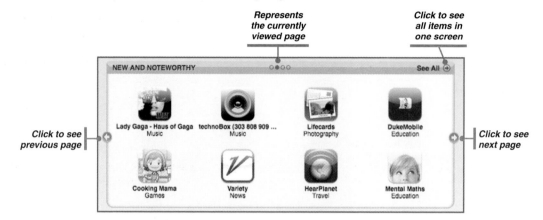

Represents the currently viewed page

Click to see all items in one screen

Click to see previous page

Click to see next page

Figure 10-1: Navigating the New and Noteworthy section of the App Store.

10. The What's Hot section displays apps that are generating a buzz in the App Store community.

11. Staff Favorites shows you what apps the good folks who work for Apple are currently smitten with.

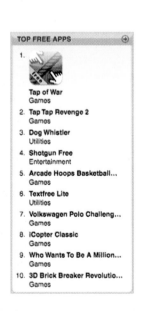

12. Quick Links gives you a few shortcuts to other items in the iTunes Store, such as a search tool and your account information.

13. Apple ranks the apps on the App Store according to how many purchases or downloads have been made for them over a certain period of time. They keep tabs on both paid and free apps.

Easily Find the Latest and Greatest Apps

The App Store has a great tool for finding apps: Power Search. You can customize your search to widen or narrow its scope, which makes it easy to find specific apps or certain types of apps.

1. To access Power Search, click its link under the Quick Links section and you will see its criteria options.

2. Applications should already be selected in the **Power Search** pop-up menu on the left side. If not, select it from the pop-up.

3. If you know part of or the entire name of a particular app, or know some words that describe its functionality, type them in the **Title/Description** field. You can also use asterisks as wildcards or just enter partial words if you don't know the exact name or term you'd like to search for.

4. Select the **Search for free applications** checkbox to limit the search to only those apps that don't cost anything more than your time.

5. If you know the name of the company that develops a particular app, enter its name in the Developer Name field.

6. Use the **Category** pop-up to search in all or only one category.

7. Choose the **Device Compatibility** pop-up to narrow the search to a particular device type, or broaden the search to include all devices.

8. Click the **Search** button to find apps that meet the criteria you've specified. Your results will display under the search criteria.

BROWSING TO QUICKLY FIND SPECIFIC APPS

If you're someone who doesn't go for fancy frills and just needs the basic ability to browse through all apps and categories, you're in luck.

1. Click the **Browse** link under the Quick Links section.

2. Select App Store in the iTunes Store pane.

3. Choose a category in the Category pane.

4. If necessary, select a subcategory in the Subcategory pane.

5. Search results will appear in the lower half of the window. Scroll up and down the list to find an item that strikes your fancy.

6. Click the small circle containing the arrow (to the right of the app name) to view the apps information page.

7. Click the **Buy App** button to purchase and/or download it.

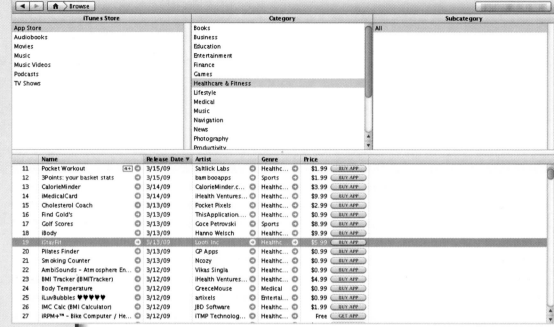

Submit Reviews of Your Favorite (and Not-So-Favorite) Apps

When you find an app that you truly enjoy, or that performs its task admirably, you should submit a review for it. Likewise, however, if you run into an app that just ridiculously underperforms, you should let the rest of the iPhone/iPod touch world know (especially if it's a paid app).

1. Use Power Search or Browse to find the app you want to review.

2. Go to the apps information page.

3. Scroll down the information page until you see the Customer Ratings section.

4. Click the **Rate this software** pop-up menu and choose a rating (1 to 5 = worst to best).

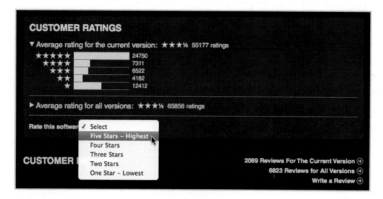

5. You must sign in to iTunes to submit the review, so enter your user name and password when prompted, and click the **Sign In** button.

6. If you want to write a detailed review, click the **Write a Review** link.

  a. Select a star rating.

  b. Enter a nickname for yourself, a title for the review, and the review contents in the appropriate fields.

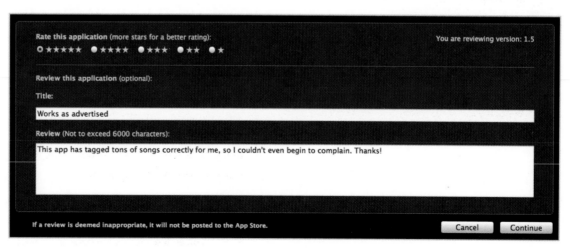

10

c. Click **Continue** to submit the review.

d. Click **Edit** to change your review, or click **Submit** to send it in.

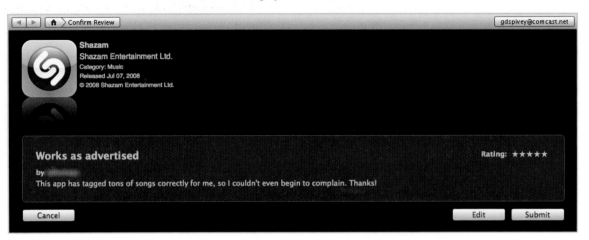

e. A member of Apple's staff will check your review before it can be posted, so it won't show up immediately. Click the **Done** button to finish the process.

Discover a Few of My Favorite Applications and Games

Finally, I'd like to share a few apps with you that I've come to find almost indispensable.

NOW PLAYING

If you love the movies, you'll love Now Playing. Now Playing is a great app for finding the newest releases, finding showtimes and what theaters a movie is playing at, watching trailers, discovering future releases, and much more. This is one movie app that has it all.

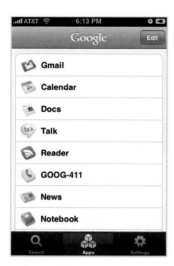

GOOGLE MOBILE APP

The Google app gives you instant access to many of Google's web applications, such as Gmail, Talk, and Calendar, right on your iPhone or iPod touch.

Another great feature with the Google app (although it's only for iPhone users) is that you can also perform a voice search for any topic! Instead of typing in a topic to search for, just speak right into your iPhone receiver, just as you would when making a call.

PANDORA

Pandora allows you to create your own Internet radio stations based on the types of music you like to listen to. Create a station using a favorite artist and Pandora will play songs by that artist and by other artists who play similar styles of music.

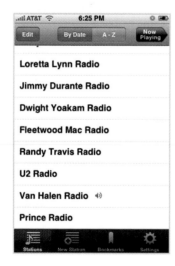

I.TV

i.TV is great for finding what's on the tube tonight, or any other night (or day) for that matter. You can view times for your favorite programs, read a synopsis of a program, read reviews, submit your own reviews, email reminders to yourself to catch a program, and much more.

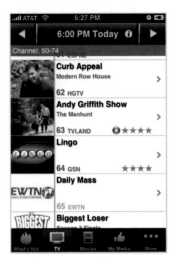

NETNEWSWIRE

If you're an RSS newsfeed junkie, NetNewsWire will keep you in the loop for all the latest news. You can add feeds and even synchronize them with the RSS reader application on your computer, which makes sure both devices are kept up-to-date.

FACEBOOK

The Facebook app is a great tool for staying in touch with friends on Facebook. You can receive notifications, emails, see photos, send messages to one another, and update your status. While not as functional as the actual Facebook Web site, the Facebook app certainly helps keep up with your account.

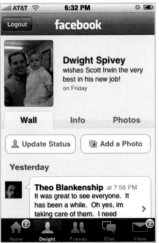

COOLIRIS

Cooliris is one of the neatest ways I've ever found to browse the Internet for pictures. You can search for any topic under the sun, and Cooliris will display the pictures it finds (using any of several available search engines) on a virtual wall. You can then flick the virtual wall with your fingers to navigate among the pictures.

BRIEFCASELITE

BriefcaseLite allows you to share files with and copy files to and from your Mac. You must have a Wi-Fi connection, and the device and your Mac will communicate through Bonjour. This is one of my must-haves!

AIM

AIM is the AOL Instant Messenger app for iPhone/iPod touch. You can use AIM just as you would on your computer, retaining your buddy list and all that good stuff. You can even use AIM to text your contacts for free! That alone is worth downloading this app and giving it a go.

AMAZON.COM

The Amazon.com app gives you a quick way to access the Amazon Web site, find books and other products, see reviews, and make purchases.

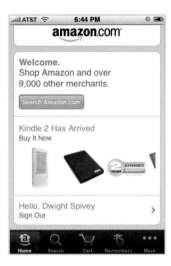

SHAZAM

Shazam is one of the coolest apps on the App Store. Ever heard a song and couldn't remember the title of it to save your firstborn's life? Never fear, Shazam is here! This app will use your iPhone's receiver to "listen" to music and will "tag" it, which is another way of saying it searches its database for the song title that matches the music. You will be amazed at how accurate this app is.

SPORTACULAR

Sportacular is my favorite way to keep up with the latest scores of my favorite team or sport. You can select from a plethora of sports, including NCAA football or basketball, the NFL or NBA, and more. You're also able to specify your favorite teams, making it a snap to instantly find out the score of the game when you just can't get to a television (or even better, be there in person).

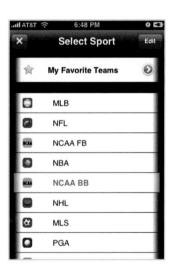

TWC (THE WEATHER CHANNEL)

The iPhone and iPod touch come with a nice weather app, but if you want a much more detailed weather forecast (for free!) you can't beat TWC. The Weather Channel app shows you current conditions, an hourly forecast, a 36-hour forecast, and 10-day forecast, maps, severe weather warnings, and more.

10

JAILBREAKING THE iPHONE/iPOD TOUCH

Jailbreaking your device sounds pretty ominous doesn't it? Most of you are probably wondering what in the world this means. Well, no fears; your iPhone or iPod touch isn't on the run from the law. To jailbreak your device means to liberate it from its dependence on the App Store as its sole means of acquiring applications. While that sounds like a great idea at first, you may want to think twice, as Apple claims it is a violation of their copyright to do so. You've been warned, and no, I won't be teaching you how to jailbreak your device here. You can find instructions for jailbreaking your device easily on the Internet, but if you turn your iPhone or iPod touch into a brick don't blame me.

WHITEPAGES

WhitePages is my favorite app for finding people and places using the iPhone. You can even perform a reverse lookup of a phone number. When you find a person or business you can call them by tapping their number on the screen, see a map of their location, and more.

Index

A

About button, tapping, 130
accounts, enabling and disabling, 136
Accounts screen, opening, 49
Action button landmark, function in Safari, 56
Address Book contacts, syncing, 21
AIM (AOL Instant Messenger) app, features of, 165
Airplane Mode, enabling and disabling, 124
Alarm function, using in Clock app, 109
albums
     adding with iPhoto, 94–95
     configuring settings for, 96
     organizing, 80
     sharing on MobilMe, 98
alerts, configuring, 128
Alltel, MMS address format for, 100
A.M., setting alarm for, 109
Amazon.com app, features of, 166
AOL Instant Messenger (AIM) app, features of, 165
app icons, stopping wiggling of, 11
app reviews, finding online, 150
App Store
     accessing Power Search in, 159
     browsing categories in, 147–148
     finding apps in, 159
     function of, 6
     interface, 155–158
     ranking of apps in, 158
     viewing hottest apps in, 147
     viewing new apps in, 146
App Store sections
     displaying, 156
     New and Noteworthy, 158
     Quick Links, 158
     Staff Favorites, 158
     What's Hot, 158
Apple cables for television, buying, 142
application settings. *See also* settings
     Mail, Contacts, Calendars, 135–138
     music and video, 141–142

Phone, 138–140
photos, 143
Safari, 140–141
applications. *See* apps
Applications pane, features of, 27–29
apps
     AIM, 165
     Amazon.com, 166
     availability of, 6
     BriefcaseLite, 165
     Calculator, 116
     Calendar, 119–120
     checking out top 25 of, 149
     Clock, 107–110
     Contacts, 120
     Cooliris, 165
     deleting from device, 153–154
     evaluating, 148
     Facebook, 164
     finding quickly, 160
     free versus paid, 148
     Google, 163
     identifying details about, 146
     installing, 150–152
     i.TV, 163–164
     Maps, 111–115
     Messages, 110–111
     NetNewsWire, 164
     Notes, 106–107
     Now Playing, 162
     opening, 7
     Pandora, 163
     reporting problems with, 151
     searching for, 150
     selecting items in, 8
     Shazam, 166
     Sportacular, 166
     Stocks, 118
     submitting reviews of, 160–162
     syncing, 154
     TWC (The Weather Channel), 166

updating currently installed, 152–153
viewing information pages for, 157
Weather, 104–106
WhitePages, 167
artists, browsing, 80
AT&T, MMS address format for, 100
attachments. *See* e-mail attachments
audio content, sorting, 80
Audio file type, extensions for, 50
audio files
     browsing, 79
     importing into iTunes, 71
audiobooks
     controlling reading speed in, 141
     organizing, 80

B

battery, charged status of, 12
battery life, saving, 124
Bcc option, using with Mail app, 137
Bluetooth button, tapping, 131
bookmarks. *See also* RSS bookmarks
     creating in Safari, 60
     deleting in Safari, 61
     editing in Safari, 62
     managing in Safari, 61–62
     opening web sites with, 61
     repositioning in Safari, 62
     synchronizing in Safari, 23, 63
Bookmarks button landmark, function
  in Safari, 56
Boost Mobile, MMS address format for, 100
BriefcaseLite app, features of, 165
brightness settings, configuring, 129
Browse link, using with apps, 160
browser pages, handling in Safari, 59
Browser window landmark, function in Safari, 56
browsing history, clearing, 140
businesses, finding with Maps app, 116

C

Calculator app
    function of, 6
    using, 116
Calendar app
    function of, 6
    using, 119–120
Calendars section, features of, 21–22
Calendars settings, configuring,
    137–138
call waiting, configuring, 138
caller ID switch, turning off, 139
calls. *See also* conference calls; incoming calls;
    phone numbers
      answering in locked mode, 33
      answering in unlocked mode, 33
      answering second, 38
      browsing recent, 41
      ending, 32–33
      going back to, 42
      incoming, 33
      making with contacts, 33
      making with keypad, 32
      placing on hold, 34, 38
      receiving, 33
      sending to voicemail, 34, 38
      switching between, 38–39
      terminating, 38
      using applications during, 42
      using keypad during, 34
      using Mute button with, 34
Calls section, configuring on Phone screen, 138
camera
    recording videos with, 86–87
    taking pictures with, 86
Camera app
    function of, 6
    viewing pictures with, 87
Camera Roll, viewing, 87
capital letter, entering on keyboard, 9

caps lock, turning on, 9
Carrier settings, appearance of, 126
Categories button, using in App Store, 147
CDs, importing from, 70
Celsius, viewing temperatures in, 105
characters
    displaying, 9
    entering on keyboard, 8
    using with letters, 10
cities, deleting in Weather app, 106
Clear options, using, 140
Clock app
    Alarm function, 109
    function of, 6
    opening, 107
    Stopwatch feature, 110
    Timer feature, 110
    using Sleep iPod option with, 110
    World Clock feature, 108
closed captioning, enabling and disabling, 142
collections, browsing, 82
.COM key in Safari, purpose of, 58
communication settings, modifying,
    130–131
compilations, organizing, 80
composers, organizing, 80
computers
    importing photos to manually, 92–94
    syncing photos with, 88–89
conference calls, creating, 39. *See also* calls
contact records, adding pictures to, 100
contacts
    adding to conference calls, 39
    adding to Favorites list, 36
    assigning photos to, 100
    assigning ringtones to, 37
    creating from recent calls, 36
    creating manually, 35
    finding, 36
    removing from Favorites list, 37
    using to make calls, 33

Contacts app
    function of, 6
    using, 120
Contacts button, functions of, 32
Contacts section, features of, 21–22
Contacts settings, configuring, 137
cookies, accepting or rejecting, 140
Cooliris app, features of, 165
Cover Flow
    browsing music with, 82
    viewing library with, 70

D

Data Roaming switch, toggling, 130
Databases button, tapping, 141
Date & Time button, using, 133
days, listing in Calendar app, 119
deleting
    apps from device, 153–154
    bookmarks in Safari, 61
    e-mail, 51–53
    e-mail accounts, 47
    icons, 11
    items from devices, 19–20
    multiple e-mails, 52
    pictures, 101
    videos, 101
device settings, resetting, 135
devices. *See also* iPhone 3G; iPod touch
    backing up before restoring, 19
    charging, 12
    copying playlists to, 77
    getting information about, 17, 130
    jailbreaking, 167
    locking and unlocking, 3–4
    naming, 21
    preventing automatic syncing with, 18–19
    registering with iTunes, 16
    removing items from, 19–20
    restoring, 18–19

saving images to in Safari, 64
synchronizing, 15–17
turning on and off, 3
viewing in iTunes, 16
dictionary, adding words to, 135
directions, getting in Maps app, 114–115
Dock, customizing icons on, 10
Documents file type, extensions for, 50

E

e-mail accounts
    adding, 44–45
    configuring, 45–46
    configuring SMTP server for, 46
    enabling and disabling, 46
    mailboxes associated with, 49
    removing, 47
    setting default for, 47
    setting messages down, 50
    storing messages for, 46
    using multiple, 47
e-mail attachments, viewing, 50–51
e-mail fonts, configuring, 54
e-mail settings, configuring, 136–137
e-mail signature, creating, 137
e-mail systems, support for, 44
e-mailing
    notes, 107
    photos and videos, 99
e-mails. *See also* Mail app
    adding signatures to, 54
    checking manually, 48
    creating, 53–54
    deleting, 51–52
    deleting multiple, 52
    displaying, 50
    displaying unread, 49
    forwarding, 53
    marking unread, 50

moving multiple, 52
pushing versus fetching, 48
replying to, 53
seeing contents of, 49–50
EQ button, using, 142
equalizers, choosing from, 142
Erase Content And Settings button, 135
Erase Data feature, using, 131
Exchange accounts, adding, 44
Exchange servers, discovering, 45

F

Facebook app, features of, 164
Fahrenheit, viewing temperatures in, 105
Favorites button, functions of, 32
Favorites list
    adding contacts to, 36
    removing contacts from, 37
fetching e-mail, 48
files, importing from, 71
folders, moving e-mails to, 52
fonts
    choosing for Mail app, 137
    configuring for e-mails, 54
forecasts, getting, 104–106

G

Genius playlists, turning on, 76
genres, organizing, 80
Google app, features of, 163
greeting, changing, 41

H

history, clearing, 140
History list
    clearing in Safari, 63
    using in Safari, 62

Hold button, using with calls, 34
Home button
    double-clicking, 8
    using, 7, 132
Home screen
    feature layout, 5
    resetting, 135
home screens
    creating, 7
    navigating between, 7
    resetting, 11
    returning to, 7
    using web clips on, 64–65

I

iCal calendars, syncing, 21
icons
    arranging, 10–11
    customizing on Dock, 10
    deleting, 11
    resetting defaults, 11
    unlocking, 10
Image Capture app, opening, 93
images. *See* photos; pictures
importing
    from CDs, 70
    from files, 71
    photos manually, 92–94
    photos to Mac, 90–91
    photos using iPhoto, 90–91
    videos manually, 92–94
incoming calls. *See also* calls
    managing multiple, 38
    sending to voicemail, 34
    silencing, 37–38
Info pane, areas of, 20–23
International Assist, toggling on and off, 138
International Keyboards button, tapping, 134
Internet radio stations, using Pandora for, 163
IP address, requesting for Wi-Fi, 125

iPhone 3G. *See also* devices
  feature layout, 2
  Ring/Silent switch on, 127
  using speaker with, 34–35
iPhone settings, configuring, 138–140
iPhoto
  adding albums with, 94–95
  importing photos with, 90–91
iPod app, function of, 6
iPod screen, sections of, 141
iPod touch. *See also* devices
  feature layout, 2
  sections of, 141
iTunes app. *See also* music; songs
  checking installation of, 14
  creating playlists in, 75
  enabling Sound Check in, 141
  formatting movies with, 77
  function of, 6
  getting, 14–15
  importing from CDs, 70
  importing from files, 71
  interface, 68–69
  opening, 18
  registering device with, 16
  support website, 68
  synchronizing playlists in, 25
  synchronizing songs in, 25
  syncing music with, 74–75
  syncing photos to computer
    with, 88–89
  syncing video with, 78–79
  using to sync albums, 94–95
  viewing device in, 16
iTunes library
  adding songs to, 71
  browsing, 79
  importing audio files into, 71
  viewing with Cover Flow, 70

iTunes Store
  App Store link in, 155
  buying movies from, 77–78
  renting movies from, 77–78
  selecting podcasts from, 73
  signing into, 143
iTunes U, accessing, 73
i.TV app, features of, 163–164

J

jailbreaking devices, 167

K

keyboard
  multiple-language, 134
  using, 8–10
Keyboard button, using, 133–134
keyboard dictionary, adding words to, 135
keypad
  making calls with, 32
  using during calls, 34

L

landmarks, functions in Safari, 56
landscape pictures, taking, 86
Language button, tapping, 134
letter keys, returning to, 9–10
library
  adding songs to, 71
  browsing, 79
  viewing with Cover Flow, 70
links, going to in Safari, 58
local businesses, finding with Maps app, 116
location services
  toggling, 131
  using, 113

location warnings, receiving, 135
locations
  bookmarking in Maps app, 113
  finding current in Map, 114
  marking with pins in Maps app, 112
  navigating in Weather app, 105–106
  viewing with Maps app, 111–112
  zooming in on in Maps, 112
locator button, using in Maps app, 114
locked mode, answering calls in, 33
locking and unlocking device, 3–4
lyrics, adding to songs, 71

M

Mac files, sharing and copying, 165
Mac OS X, importing photos with, 93–94
Macs, importing photos to, 90–91
Mail Accounts section, features of, 21, 23
Mail app. *See also* e-mails
  choosing fonts for, 137
  function of, 6
  opening, 47
  opening to Accounts screen, 49
Mail settings, configuring, 136–137
mailboxes
  associating with e-mail accounts, 49
  moving e-mails to, 52
Maps app
  bookmarking locations in, 113
  dropping pins to mark locations, 112
  finding current location in, 114
  finding local businesses with, 116
  function of, 6
  getting directions in, 114–115
  locator button in, 114
  setting traffic conditions, 115
  viewing locations with, 111–112

messages. *See* e-mails
Messages app
    features of, 99–100
    using, 110–111
Microsoft Exchange accounts, adding, 44
MMS (Multimedia Messaging Service), using to send
  multimedia, 99–100
MobileMe
    features of, 21
    overview of, 21
    sharing albums on, 98
    trying for free, 95
MobileMe accounts, adding, 44
MobileMe gallery
    adding photos to, 95–97
    adding videos to, 95–97
months, listing in Calendar app, 119
More button, tapping, 80
Move button, using with e-mails, 52
movies
    buying from iTunes Store, 77–78
    formatting with iTunes, 77
    Now Playing app for, 162
    renting from iTunes Store, 77–78
    synchronizing, 25
MP3 files, importing into iTunes, 71
multimedia, sending via MMS, 99–100
music. *See also* iTunes; songs
    browsing with Cover Flow, 82
    music, managing manually, 18–20
    modifying playback for, 141–142
    playing with slideshows, 99
    syncing with iTunes, 74–75
Music app, function of, 6
Music pane, features of, 25
Mute button, using with calls, 34

N

NetNewsWire app, features of, 164
Network button, tapping, 130–131

network requests, ending for Wi-Fi, 126
network settings, resetting, 135
New Mail button, tapping, 54
newsfeeds. *See* RSS newsfeeds
Next button landmark, function in Safari, 56
Nike + iPod app, function of, 6
Notes app
    function of, 6
    using, 106–107
notifications, viewing, 126–127
Now Playing app, features of, 162
numbers, displaying, 9

O

on and off, turning device, 3
onscreen keyboard, using, 8–10

P

Pages button landmark, function in Safari, 56
Pandora app, features of, 163
passcode
    assigning, 132
    using, 4–5
Passcode Lock button, tapping, 131
Password Lock, using, 4
passwords
    assigning to voicemail, 139
    using with voicemail, 40
people, finding via WhitePages, 167
Phone app
    function of, 6
    opening, 32
phone calls. *See* calls
phone functionality, initiating, 32
phone numbers. *See also* calls
    calling on web pages, 65
    entering, 32
Phone settings, configuring for iPhone, 138–140
photo albums. *See* albums

photos. *See also* pictures
    adding to MobileMe gallery, 95–97
    assigning to contacts, 100
    e-mailing, 99
    importing manually, 92–94
    importing to Mac, 90–91
    selecting, 92
    syncing with computer, 88–89
Photos app
    function of, 6
    viewing pictures with, 88
Photos button, using with slideshows, 143
Photos pane, using, 26
Picture file type, extensions for, 50
pictures. *See also* photos
    adding to contact records, 100
    advisory about deletion of, 101
    browsing Internet for, 165
    deleting, 101
    downloading, 94
    organizing into albums, 94–95
    saving to device in Safari, 64
    scrolling through, 87
    selecting for wallpaper, 130
    setting as wallpaper, 100–101
    taking with camera, 86
    viewing in e-mail attachments, 51
    viewing with Camera app, 87
    viewing with Photos app, 88
PIN (personal identification number), using with
  SIM card, 139
pins in Maps app, marking locations with, 112
playback controls, using, 81
playlists
    browsing, 79
    copying to devices, 77
    creating in iTunes, 75
    Genius, 76
    Smart, 76
    synchronizing in iTunes, 25

P.M., setting alarm for, 109
podcasts
    downloading, 81
    organizing, 80
    subscribing to, 29, 72–74
Podcasts pane, features of, 27
Power Search, accessing in App Store, 159
Previous button landmark, function in Safari, 56
pushing e-mail, 48

R

radio stations, using Pandora for, 163
reading speed, controlling in audiobooks, 141
recent calls, browsing, 41
Recents button, functions of, 32
Record button, using with voice memos, 121
Region Format button, tapping, 134
reminders, creating with voice memos, 121
Renew Lease button, using with Wi-Fi, 125
Reply/Forward button, using with e-mails, 53
Reset button, using, 134–135
Restore option, function of, 18
restoring devices, 18–19
Restrictions button, using, 132
reviews, submitting for apps, 160–162
Reviews button, using with apps, 151
Ring/Silent switch, using on iPhone, 127
ringtones
    assigning to contacts, 37
    creating, 26–27
    selecting, 128
    silencing, 38
    synchronizing with iPhone, 23–24
Route button, using in Maps app, 114
RSS bookmarks, organizing, 63. *See also* bookmarks
RSS newsfeeds
    app for, 164
    using in Safari, 63

S

Safari app
    choosing default search engine for, 59–60
    clearing History list in, 63
    closing web pages in, 59
    creating bookmarks in, 60
    deleting bookmarks in, 61
    downloading, 63
    editing bookmarks in, 62
    function of, 6
    handling browser pages in, 59
    managing bookmarks in, 61–62
    navigating web pages in, 58–59
    opening web pages in, 59
    opening web sites in, 59
    repositioning bookmarks ion, 62
    saving images to devices in, 64
    stopping web pages from loading in, 58
    synchronizing bookmarks in, 23, 63
    using History list in, 62
    using RSS feeds in, 63
    viewing Web pages in, 56–57
    zooming in and out of pages in, 58
Safari keyboard, .COM key on, 58
Safari landmarks, functions of, 56
Safari settings, configuring, 140–141
satellite images, viewing, 112–113
scientific calculator, accessing, 116
screen shots, taking, 101
scrolling up and down, 7–8
Search button, using with apps, 159
search engine, choosing for Safari, 59–60
Search field landmark, function in Safari, 56
searching
    for apps, 150
    for items, 121
security, customizing, 5
Send button, using with e-mails, 53
settings. *See also* application settings

Airplane Mode, 124
brightness, 129
Carrier, 126
communication, 130–131
Fetch New Data, 126
General, 130–135
Sounds, 127–128
VPN, 126
wallpaper, 129
Wi-Fi, 124–125
Settings app
    configuring music settings with, 141–142
    configuring phone settings with, 138–140
    configuring photos with, 143
    configuring Safari settings with, 140–141
    configuring video settings with, 141–142
    function of, 6
    General options, 130–135
Shazam app, features of, 166
SHIFT key, activating, 9
Short Messaging Service (SMS), 99
signatures, adding to e-mails, 54, 137
Silent, setting iPhone to, 127
SIM card, locking with PIN, 139
Sleep iPod option, using with Clock app, 110
Sleep/Wake button
    using, 3–5
    using to silence ringtones, 38
slideshows
    choosing transitions for, 143
    playing music with, 99
    repeating, 143
    setting preferences for, 99
    using Photos button with, 143
    viewing, 98
    viewing randomly, 143
Smart Playlists, creating, 76
SMS (Short Messaging Service), 99
SMTP server, configuring for e-mail, 46
songs. *See also* iTunes; music

adding lyrics to, 71
adding to library, 71
browsing, 80
finding titles of, 166
jumping back to, 79
managing manually, 19–20
synchronizing in iTunes, 25
Sound Check feature, enabling and disabling, 141
sound settings, configuring, 127–128
speaker
using with iPhone, 34–35
using with visual voicemail, 40
Sportacular app, features of, 166
Sprint, MMS address format for, 100
Stocks app
function of, 6
using, 118
Stopwatch feature, using in Clock app, 110
Summary pane
customizing sync options in, 17–18
options in, 18
symbols, accessing on keyboard, 9
Sync option, using with apps, 154
sync options
configuring in Info pane, 20–23
setting, 17–18
synchronizing devices, 15–17

T

Task menu, using with web pages, 65
television, watching videos on, 142
temperatures, viewing in F or C, 105
Text app, function of, 6
text messages
choosing alert for, 128
previewing, 141
sending, 99–100
thumbnail image, tapping, 87
Timer feature, using in Clock app, 110
T-Mobile, MMS address format for, 100

To/Cc field, configuring for e-mail, 137
toolbar, configuring, 82
Top 25 button, using with apps, 149
touchscreen, navigating with, 7–8
traffic conditions, setting in Maps app, 115
transitions, choosing for slideshows, 143
Trash
emptying, 52–53
sending e-mail to, 51
TTY machine, using iPhone with, 139
turning device on and off, 3
TV shows, synchronizing, 25
TWC (The Weather Channel) app, features of, 166

U

Update option, function of, 18
Updates button, using with apps, 152
URL field
entering web addresses in, 57–58
landmark in Safari, 56
Usage button, pressing, 130
USB hub, recognizing, 94
User Account Control, flashing, 15

V

Verizon, MMS address format for, 100
videos
adding to MobileMe gallery, 95–97
deleting, 101
e-mailing, 99
importing manually, 92–94
importing to Mac, 90–91
managing manually, 18–20
modifying playback for, 141–142
recording with camera, 86–87
syncing with iTunes, 78–79

watching, 83
watching on television, 143
watching with YouTube, 117
Videos app, function of, 6
Videos pane, features of, 25
Vista, importing photos with, 92–93
visual voicemail, utilizing, 40–41
voice memos, creating reminders with, 121
voicemail
assigning password to, 139
sending incoming calls to, 34, 38
using passwords with, 40
visual, 40–41
Voicemail button, functions of, 32
volume
adjusting, 11, 128
adjusting with Sound Check, 141
volume limit, setting, 142
VPN (virtual private network), using, 131
VPN button, appearance of, 126

W

wallpaper
configuring settings for, 129
finding on Web, 130
selecting pictures for, 130
setting pictures as, 100–101
WAV files, importing into iTunes, 71
Weather app
adding locations in, 104–105
deleting cities in, 106
function of, 6
navigating locations in, 105–106
using, 104
viewing temperatures in, 105
The Weather Channel (TWC) app, features of, 166
web addresses, entering in URL field, 57–58
Web Browser section, features of, 23

web clips, using on home screen, 64–65
web pages
    Apple cables for television, 142
    calling phone numbers on, 65
    closing in Safari, 59
    displaying number open in Safari, 59
    navigating in Safari, 58–59
    opening in Safari, 59
    reloading in Safari, 58
    viewing in Safari, 56–57
web sites
    app reviews, 150
    iTunes support, 68

MobileMe trial account, 95
    opening in Safari, 59
    opening with bookmarks, 61
    specialized, 57
    wallpaper, 130
WhitePages app, features of, 167
Wi-Fi settings
    configuring, 124–125
    ending network requests for, 126
Windows Vista, importing photos with,
    92–93
word key, tapping, 134
World Clock feature, using, 108

Y

YouTube
    app, 6
    watching videos on, 117

Z

zooming in and out, 8, 58